"I could not put the book down, and I cried and smiled through it. I pray that this book will land in the hands of every mother who has gone through the things I have gone through so she can know that she is not alone. This book should be shared with anyone who has lost a child no matter the age or cause. Anyone who has suffered a significant loss of any kind will really benefit from reading it. *Life from the Ashes* is truly helpful and healing. I feel so much better and exceptionally blessed to have read it!"

JENNIE GONZALES
Bereaved Mother; Santa Fe, New Mexico

"When we are forced to travel a grief journey that goes way beyond our knowing or comprehension, we desperately need help and guidance. Having that come from a mom who is walking that grief path herself, creates a powerful and deeply authentic resource for the bereaved. Shari shares her journey of pain, confusion, insights, taking care of oneself, spiritual awareness, as well as unmistakable and profound signs from her son. There is much to learn on this most difficult journey, and Shari opens up her heart to readers with a deep desire to help them find their way to greater understanding and healing. As a bereaved mom myself, I know *Life from the Ashes* is truly a gift of love and healing."

SARA RUBLE
Bereaved Mother, Teacher and Speaker; Stow, Ohio

T0161804

"*Life from the Ashes* contains so many great strategies for coping with major trauma or loss and for finding a way to hope again. These strategies can be applied to many types of losses. Shari is a true inspiration. I was in tears at the dedication."

PAM RUPPA
Teacher; Milwaukee, Wisconsin

"This autobiography is a heroine's journey through deep despair to spiritual awakening. Shari recalls her most painful moments of family loss while sharing intimate moments of Divine connection through which she found new meaning. *Life from the Ashes* offers hope to all those who have experienced great loss and who wish to transform their pain into purpose. Shari shows us how we can choose to live a more meaningful and purposeful life after loss."

CARL BROOKS
Business Coach; Amsterdam, The Netherlands

"*Life from the Ashes* provides wisdom and hope for all who have endured great loss, particularly the unspeakable pain of losing a child. The strength and grace Shari shows is inspirational, and her story has changed me forever. I have a new, deeply spiritual and lifelong appreciation for each day of my life and those of my loved ones. I am thankful Shari opened her heart and soul through writing this and gave me the priceless gift of being more present in my own life each and every day."

KATHY GREER
Albuquerque, New Mexico

"I read *Life from the Ashes* in one sitting and found myself reflecting on what is important in life and why gratitude is the key to happiness. What I found so hopeful was the path Shari describes to find peace and joy through gratitude. We spend our lives searching for this and often don't know how to find it. I loved the book and would highly recommend it. I am a believer in signs…it happens to me."

ANNE GROVE
Charlotte, North Carolina

"Everyone who has suffered a devastating loss will want to read *Life from the Ashes*. This book will light their way through the dark and encourage their broken heart. Having read this book, I am full of new hope. I have come to believe that the love we shared with those who have passed on remains, grows, and will in time help comfort and guide us. I'm sure there is more, and I eagerly await Vol. 2!"

TRISH NICKERSON
Director at Cottonwood School; Corrales, New Mexico

Life from the Ashes

life from the Ashes

Finding Signs of Hope After Loss

Shari O'Loughlin

NEW YORK

LONDON • NASHVILLE • MELBOURNE • VANCOUVER

Life from the Ashes

Finding Signs of Hope After Loss

© 2018 Shari O'Loughlin

All rights reserved. No portion of this book may be reproduced, stored in a retrieval system, or transmitted in any form or by any means—electronic, mechanical, photocopy, recording, scanning, or other—except for brief quotations in critical reviews or articles, without the prior written permission of the publisher.

Published in New York, New York, by Morgan James Publishing in partnership with Difference Press. Morgan James is a trademark of Morgan James, LLC. www.MorganJamesPublishing.com

The Morgan James Speakers Group can bring authors to your live event. For more information or to book an event visit The Morgan James Speakers Group at www.TheMorganJamesSpeakersGroup.com.

ISBN 9781683507314 paperback
ISBN 9781683507321 eBook
Library of Congress Control Number: 2017912966

Cover and Interior Design by:
Chris Treccani
www.3dogcreative.net

In an effort to support local communities, raise awareness and funds, Morgan James Publishing donates a percentage of all book sales for the life of each book to Habitat for Humanity Peninsula and Greater Williamsburg.

Get involved today! Visit
www.MorganJamesBuilds.com

DEDICATION

Dedicated to my beloved son, Connor,
who showed me the way;

and to my amazing daughters, MacKenzie & Erin,
for giving me a reason to want one.

TABLE OF CONTENTS

FOREWORD

Life from the Ashes is a stirring, painful, but important read. While most of us never have to experience the deep anguish of losing a child, all of us must learn how to process the smallest disappointments to the most profound losses. We do this by living through the vicissitudes of grief. And when we do this well, the transformative result is wisdom.

Shari takes us with her on her journey through devastating loss and the subsequent shocks that accompany her grief - feelings of abandonment, fear, guilt, loss of control, and sometimes, hopelessness. There is a Buddhist saying, "When you burn, burn yourself completely." Shari burned. Stay with her through the discomfort, however, to see what unfolds from that pain, something that can unfold for each of us when we experience our own losses if we are willing to persevere and see what awaits us on the other side.

When we are willing to explore the depths of our darkness rather than avoiding or numbing it, the evolution of our spirit unfolds, and we awaken to the eternal spiritual beings that we are. I am thrilled that Shari has shared her story so that others can see and know the healing that results from accessing and finding a spiritual foundation for creating new life after trauma. This knowledge can help so many in our world who are bereft for decades after such a loss and left feeling imprisoned by emptiness. This awareness of life in its fullness, ever-ongoing, is wisdom.

I am honored to write this foreword given my lifelong work with grief in my psychotherapy practice and knowing Shari personally as she has made this journey she did not choose but boldly faced. My experience in working with many individuals suffering from traumatic loss has led me to believe what these clients tell me - that true healing is only possible within a context of some kind of spiritual foundation. I am not speaking of a specific religious community or one specific religious doctrine that speaks to death and what comes after this life. I am speaking about one's own personal spiritual connectedness to that which is beyond us here physically and speaks to our highest selves as we evolve, transform, and live. The most common and suffocating feeling from deep loss is the lack of control we experience, particularly as a parent unable to prevent harm and the death of a child. We cannot change those experiences that devastate and tumultuously change our lives. What we can control is what we choose to do after the loss and the spiritual path we seek or stumble upon to show us the way.

Shari interweaves throughout the book both her physical path of loss, mourning, and bereavement with her spiritual and transformational journey that, I believe, is birthed from such loss. What remains unspoken, but the reader can clearly feel by the end, is the greater purpose and deeper meaning of living that Shari learns and embodies from this dreadful journey and unexpected transformation.

What may surprise you are the beautiful stories woven throughout Shari's painful journey that illuminate her spiritual awakening and her profound connection with her son, Connor, in spirit. I frequently hear these remarkable stories from my clients, and many more people can benefit from knowing that this spiritual connection is truly possible. The reader can feel how the bond between Shari and Connor in life transfers to an equally beautiful but different connection in spirit. Her stories give us desperately-needed hope that there really is something more than we may believe or that we slow down long enough to see in our frenetic world. It is the hope that I think so many of us are afraid to speak of for fear it is out of reach, unrealistic, or a myth. It is the understanding that spiritual connectedness and grounding can come to each of us individually when we choose paths in our life that allow them to enter.

You will find camaraderie and kinship in the journey Shari shares. Her journey can apply to many of the losses we experience in our lives including death of a loved one, loss of a job or business, financial ruin, divorce, health problems, loss of spiritual connectedness and hope, or the terrorism and violence we see happening too frequently around us. You will learn practical and beneficial strategies for healing and moving forward from any loss and from the disillusionment and pain we experience in our lives. Her illumination of gratitude, mindfulness in living, and seeking greater meaning beyond our daily activities is completely inspiring.

Prepare to be changed by reading *Life from the Ashes*. Keep this book close at hand. You will likely want to read it a second time or re-read certain sections that speak personally to you. Whether or not you have experienced a similar devastating loss, you will relate to much that is shared here, both the painful as well as the hopeful and healing. You will be touched at your deepest level by journeying through one of the greatest losses a person can experience in life, which Shari has graciously and authentically invited us in to know. And you will be inspired and moved beyond what you might hope for by learning of her spiritual journey that ran right alongside her dark and painful grief path, providing illumination and hope for all of us. Your capacity for compassion, empathy, and assisting others in pain will have grown by the time you have finished reading. Enjoy this practical, spiritual, transformational, and inspirational work that we can apply to our own lives in order to transform and reach higher possibilities within ourselves and with others with whom we share this life journey.

Gail Carr Feldman, PhD
Clinical Psychologist, Author, Professional Coach
Albuquerque, New Mexico, U.S.A.

PREFACE

This book is about the loss of my son and my journey of grief, but I want to acknowledge all three of the loving people who were killed in the accident on July 26, 2012. My son, Connor O'Loughlin Mantsch, was with one of his best friends, Connor Porter, and Connor Porter's father, Patrick Porter. Both of our families suffered immense losses on that day as did all of the people in this world they collectively touched. Connor and Connor were great friends. Both of them were high-spirited and funny, big-hearted and always smiling, and they had peaceful, gentle souls. All three are loved and missed by so many.

Shari O'Loughlin

INTRODUCTION

The first year of traumatic grief can be quite a blur. In the early days and weeks after loss, many people are around to tell you what to do next, assist you in making difficult decisions, help you accomplish basic tasks, and remind you to eat, drink, and shower. They also help as best they can with the arduous and abhorrent tasks that are required immediately after a tragedy.

After the early stages, people remain helpful but are not so regularly by your side. Support, resources, and guides are available to help you make it through the next hour, the next day, and the next week. Nothing feels easy during the first year. Each day and new experience can feel like one assault on top of another. There are so many "firsts" to face that you likely never thought about before. There is the first of any holiday without your child. The first major holiday that your extended family gathers together for with one less child. The first guitar or band concert you watch at school that no longer includes a chair occupied by your child. Your child's birthday and then your first birthday without him. Your first trip away as a smaller family, or the first time you visit your family's favorite restaurant and must ask for a smaller table. The email that is errantly sent to you as a parent in the grade you no longer have a child in. Or the day your family celebrates a special occasion for one of your other children such as graduation or a wedding.

Each one of these is a new loss, and it takes every ounce of energy to get through each one of them. After all of this heartache and work, it feels like something should be different at the end of the first year. You have made it through one of the toughest battles a person or God could ask of you. The reward must be a reprieve of some sort like feeling less pain or remembering more of the good memories of your loved one's life instead of the awful ones of his or her death. Perhaps you hope to have a true belly laugh again someday without feeling guilt or wonder how to feel like this new family you have been given with one less person can feel right.

But the harsh reality on day 366 is that nothing really feels much different. It still feels like the most awful burden to bear, and at the same time, it feels like all of your resources have been depleted just in trying to make it through all of those firsts. This reality can feel crushing. It is impossible to imagine that all of what it took to get through that first year must be done again, and again, and again with no real great reward because you are still living without your child. You likely still question whether you will ever feel happiness again like you felt before and worry whether your other children will make it through okay. You may question if you will feel like a competent parent or a caring, whole professional again. You may wonder whether your new, smaller family with its gaping hole can feel like a whole family again. Many times you have heard that time heals all wounds. That suggestion may help very little because you don't feel any better with the time that has passed, and at times you feel worse now that the shock has worn off and the reality of this lifetime without your child or loved one is clearer. You do not feel like waiting for time to just keep passing and hoping you will somehow feel better someday.

I have walked this painful journey and share your pain. I have experienced being asked to live a new life I did not choose and did not want. Many of the steps on my journey were not conscious to me at the time, especially in the early days. They were steps to get me merely to the next hour or next day, and those were painfully hard. I wrote this book to share my journey of faith and hope, parts of which I consciously chose and parts I stumbled upon. It is a journey I would have never thought possible and would have questioned if someone described it to me years before. But I have lived it and now possess a more resilient foundation to live the rest of my life without my son, Connor, while experiencing a stronger spirituality and connection to something greater. It has given me a daily connection to Connor and God that has increased my faith and hope while giving me the courage to truly seek happiness and joy in my life again, in honor of Connor's life and without guilt.

When I use the term God or any other, I am referring to whatever feels true to you whether you use the term God, Creator, Higher Power, Source, Lord, Divine, Inner Wisdom, Higher Self, Spirit, Universe, or any other. There is no one "right" meaning, and it is not my intention to exclude anyone's beliefs. I use the terms that feel most true to me and most easily describable in those places, and at times I may use different ones. Please use the name that feels most true to you whenever I make these references throughout the book.

This book is a story of hope and healing that grew from loss. First, I share my story and then move into the process I followed to find healing and initiate steps to rebuild my life. While there is no one path through grief and loss, I learned that there is a general process a person can use when facing this journey. The steps I share are as follows: acknowledging the new life you did not choose; acknowledging the changed person you are becoming; creating space for something new; learning how to feel your loved one is still with you; encouraging more signs and connection; fostering changes for deeper living; and discovering a spiritual foundation for healing.

It has now been five years since we lost our beautiful Connor. Those five years have seemed like at least 20, and it is sometimes hard to remember much of who I was before the accident. In these five years I have come to find that this new me is not only a shell of loss as I once painfully feared. Because of the many blessings I have received from people and the Universe along this path, I have a stronger foundation on which to stand and greater clarity about how to live vibrantly, more meaningfully, and very deeply. My wish for you after reading *Life from the Ashes*, is that you will have more strategies to help face significant loss, know new ways to comfort your pain, experience greater healing, and feel hope and beauty again in your life.

PART ONE

My Story

CHAPTER 1

Before

"There are only two ways to live your life.
One is as though nothing is a miracle.
The other is as though everything is a miracle."
~ Albert Einstein

Our family has always been very active, and we love travelling to different places. While we have enjoyed many elaborate seaside and adventure vacations, we have also enjoyed the simplicity and peace that comes from camping in nature. We started camping with our children when they were very young. Our kids enjoyed almost every part of it except the unpacking and cleanup. They loved the darkness and all of the stars that are not possible to see when near a city. They loved the special meals that broke household rules of nutrition and proper times of day so they could chase treasures in nature. They loved the s'mores, toast made on a stick, and hauling water for dishes washed in a bucket. Most of all they loved the closeness of our family being together for most of the day and sleeping all together in one tent at night.

We had not been camping for a number of years and almost didn't make the Fourth of July long weekend trip. Life was very hard for quite some time due to the economic recession's effect on our family business and my return to full-time outside work that it necessitated. Getting organized for a camping trip was a lot harder at this stage than it had been years earlier.

I told MacKenzie, Connor, and Erin that we had to leave within a three-hour window if we hoped to find an open campsite somewhere during the busy holiday weekend. If everyone pitched in, I thought we could do it. This trip would be impromptu and less organized than our usual trips. Because the kids wanted to go so badly, they were more than willing to help. We each had our assignments and worked together to make it happen.

I set to work googling campgrounds within a three or four-hour driving distance. Bryan set about looking at our minivan to figure out what it might need to be ready for the trip. The kids worked together to find our camping items that were still in boxes after our recent move and were not particularly well-marked or stored together in the same place. Connor was especially diligent in the hunt because he loved nature and the outdoors so much. He had turned 14 just two months prior and was thankfully bigger and stronger to help lug and haul things from the boxes and bins to the car.

There was no time for a trip to the grocery store, so we took whatever food and drinks we had in the house. Things were tucked and shoved into every available space in the van quite quickly, including the five of us and our large dog, her bed, and her big food bag. A little less than four hours later we arrived at probably the only open campsite left in northern New Mexico or southern Colorado on one of the most popular holiday camping weekends. Thankfully, the place we found in Pegosa Springs, Colorado, was beautiful.

We had the normal chaos that is typical of a family with two adults, two teenagers, a pre-teen, and an 85-pound dog all tossed together in a van and then in a tent. There were arguments of who went first, who went where, and who was getting the better or worse spot. But we also had the beautiful time, space, and sharing of a family who was away from the rush and heavy scheduling of everyday life while spending time together in the peaceful tranquility of nature.

On July 3rd, Bryan and I took a morning walk with our dog, Asia, along a wide gravel road with many farms and homes spread far apart. While walking back, we had a curious incident that began when we heard a faint, female voice calling for help from somewhere far off in the distance. As we darted around to determine what we could be hearing, we saw a very old woman way on the other end of a long gravel driveway. She had fallen out of her wheelchair while picking fruit from her tree. She was a sturdy older woman who had lived many years and had probably experienced a lot in her long life. After we helped her back into her wheelchair bruised and bleeding a little, she wanted to chat. We talked a short time about the normal things one discusses with a new acquaintance including her husband, who was away working the farm, her kids and grandkids, our camping weekend, and our family. When she asked us how many children we had, we told her about our three kids, their names, genders, and ages. Her immediate comment was quite curious. She said, "It is good that you have three children in case you ever lose one." We became quiet and paused a bit at the comment. We finished the conversation, wished her well, and completed our walk back to our campsite and the kids. When we talked about it on the walk back to our site, we were both very surprised and caught off guard by her words. Then we figured that it was not such an unusual comment for someone in her early 90's who lived through a time when losing a child was more common. It lingered with us for days, though. Once back home, we asked our friends who had three children if they had ever received that comment. None of them had, and they were all very surprised.

I had planned to go for a run when I returned from our walk since I regularly exercised but had not had the chance to get out in a few days. I was surprised to find a strange muscle strain on the inside of my right knee. I had not recalled injuring it, so I was quite perplexed. But it was a visible red line that burned and caused me pain. I was irritated as I have to plan my exercise pretty strategically with my very busy work and family schedule. After grumbling a bit, I resigned myself to the fact that it was a mystery I didn't have the energy or time to figure out. At that time the girls wanted to go horseback riding and Connor wanted to do one of his favorite things, which was to fish. A good fishing lake was not easily accessible since we lived in a city in the desert of New Mexico. Bryan suggested that I take Connor fishing since I did not get to do that very often, and he would take MacKenzie and Erin horseback riding. That sounded great and I agreed.

The fishing itself was not good and Connor had no bites. He was not happy about this part since he liked to have results catching a few big fish by the end of his time spent on the shore. But we talked and shared a lot and ate munchies and things that I normally didn't indulge in, which included his favorite lime flavored Tostitos chips and a bag of M&M's. We munched, talked, laughed, and shared time while I observed how tranquil and serene he was when he was in nature doing the things he loved. By now I was glad that I had not been able to go for that run and appreciated the special moments we were sharing.

After having no bites on his fishing line for quite a while, Connor wanted to explore a nearby swamp where he found great success catching crawfish. He was a muddy mess but was fascinated and so enthused with this unexpected treasure we discovered. I followed him around and shared his excitement looking at all of the specimens, taking photos, and getting my feet wet and dirty as I sunk into the muck on the sides of the muddy pond. I tried to be as adventurous as I could, but I stopped short of fully walking into the muddy swamp with him or holding the squiggling, pinching crawfish.

We all returned to the campsite after the different activities and continued to enjoy many natural and simple pleasures that weekend. Connor taught Erin how to brew natural tea by picking edible herbs like mint, dandelion, and clover, then brewing them in water over the campfire. Connor loved to chop firewood and make campfires, so he happily took on the role of fire master for the weekend. We all shared the work involved such as cooking meals, cleaning dishes, walking Asia and picking up after her, and making sure the cooler stayed cold. We experienced the normal share of bickering and complaining that happens when a family travels together. But in the end, we enjoyed a wonderful respite together away from the activities that pull everyone in different directions each day. It was simple but rejuvenating for all of us, and I was so glad that we all worked hard to make it happen.

After we returned from the holiday weekend, the next few weeks were full of fairly typical family activities. I had a business trip to Chicago that was interesting but took time away from my family during the precious last weeks of summer. Connor attended a soccer camp at the University of New Mexico that was very fun for him since he got to train with the college players. MacKenzie had obtained her first summer job working at a children's day care center, and Erin was attending a variety of interesting camps during the remaining weeks of summer.

Connor was one of three friends named Connor in their grade of 160 students at school, and they would all be starting their freshman year of high school shortly. In order to differentiate at school, one of the Connors was called Connor, and our Connor and Connor Porter were each called by their last names, Mantsch and Porter. They laughed at this and liked this way of distinguishing between the three.

On Sunday, July 22ⁿᵈ, I received a call from Connor Porter's dad, Pat. He asked whether Connor could join him and his Connor on a trip to Sedona for the next few days. Pat was an experienced pilot who owned a plane and had flown for many years. He liked to take a trip each year with each of his children and one of their friends to have a special time doing unique things each child enjoyed. The plan was to leave from the Albuquerque private airport early Monday morning. The flight would take about an hour and 15 minutes, and they would arrive in time to have breakfast at the Sedona airport, which was Pat's tradition. They would spend Monday, Tuesday, and Wednesday doing fun activities and return sometime on Thursday.

I was nervous about this call but could not identify or articulate why. Some of the reasons would seem normal for most any parent. I had not flown in a private plane before, I had not seen the airport before, and of course I worried about Connor going on a trip like that without us. A mother worries when her child rides with someone else to his soccer game, and this was a trip on an airplane. On the other hand, we had been to Sedona several times, and Bryan and I were quite familiar with the city. We really enjoyed Sedona and knew that Connor would love this type of trip. Pat liked to do many of the adventurous outdoor activities that Connor loved, and Connor was always happiest in nature.

I was hoping when I spoke with Connor that he would be unsure about it or feel a little uncomfortable with such a last minute request. Not surprisingly, Connor was ecstatic and could have cared less about the things on my mind. He begged me to be able to go. Bryan and I then discussed it in detail. As we went back and forth, I was kind of hoping he would come up with a very clear and practical reason why it was not a good idea. As we talked further, neither of us could come up with a very good reason to say no. Connor's schedule was uncommonly clear that week, and he would just miss two of the weekly pre-season high school soccer practices that preceded tryouts. Since he had been at those consistently all month, that was not a big problem. Soccer camp at the University was finished as were his summer activities and camps at the school. His schedule was so unusually open that he would have likely been bored and sitting around a lot if he stayed home.

Bryan and I seemed to share an unspoken level of uncertainty that neither of us could quite pinpoint. This discomfort seemed like fairly normal parental concern under the circumstances. I spoke with Connor more to see what we should do. I was honest and upfront with him. We were very close and could often read one another without speaking any words, so we did not have problems understanding one another or communicating. I told him that his schedule was open, and I recognized how interested he was in going, but we were hesitant. As we spoke, I could see Connor's heart singing and his spirit craving this opportunity. He said, "Mom, I have this unique opportunity to do this, and it really, really means the world to me. Please let me go." At that moment our eyes and hearts connected and we agreed.

I called Pat to tell him our answer. Then Connor and I began to pack his things, which was fun. He was much more enthused to pack for a trip like this than most, and I enjoyed watching how excited he was to go. He was by nature a minimalist, and this worked great as Pat asked us to pack light and keep it very simple. They would pick up anything they needed that was forgotten. Connor was a typical teenaged guy and easily interpreted that statement to mean forgoing any changes of clothes, showering items, etc. He loved backcountry camping and could happily postpone changes of clothes or cleaning rituals for when the fun was over. His bigger concern was that he wanted to take a large number of pocket knives, which he collected and considered precious and dear. He always knew why he might need this one in this circumstance and this other one in another circumstance. We discussed, negotiated, and settled on a medium-sized duffle bag containing his three favorite shirts, three favorite shorts, just a few of his most special pocket knives, and a limited number of necessary toiletries and personal items. He took the book that he was reading over the summer, which was *War and Peace*. He took his iPod touch with all of his movies and music plus his phone. To top it off, he took his favorite hat that he had gotten as a gift the previous Christmas, which was his Green Bay Packer Super Bowl Championship XLV cap that he wore all the time.

Connor was ecstatic, and we proceeded with a normal night. I wish I could say that we somehow made that Sunday evening, our last together, a monumental night. Had we known what was to come, we surely would have. But we didn't know. There was nothing special or hugely different. We did our usual Sunday night routine, which was family pizza and movie night. It was a simple and small ritual but very special to our family. The idea of this on Sunday evenings was twofold. It gave us something special to do before we all started the work and school week instead of just focusing on laundry, yard work, and homework. And it gave incentive for everyone to get their work done earlier in the weekend to enjoy this time of relaxation, togetherness, and fun. So that it stayed simple for me, the menu was pizza from Papa Murphy's and my "famous" and well-loved Greek salad. We rotated each week, and whoever had their turn got to choose the movie and the type of pizza. We always added popcorn, and we guarded Sunday evenings carefully to keep the time open for what was important family time. The movie we watched that night was "We Bought a Zoo." In that movie a father and his children work to build a new life after the mother passes away. I reflected later on how prophetic that was for our family's last movie night all together.

When Monday morning came, Connor was to be picked up at 6:20 a.m. I got up at about 5:45 to help him get ready. We packed Connor's last minute items, and I could see how much he was anticipating the enjoyable days ahead. He did not like to get up early, which is pretty typical for teenaged boys, so we rarely saw him enthusiastic for anything at 6:15 in the morning. This morning was surely an exception and reflected how important this trip was to him.

I never had any idea that this was the last time I would ever look into my beautiful son's eyes, that I would ever hug and hold my boy, or that I would ever smell his unique and familiar scent. These few parting moments were not momentous. We have them many times with our children as they grow up and go off to do this or that with others while coming right back home with a great experience to tell afterward. Bryan and I said our goodbyes, and I said some last words from mother to son about best behavior and good decisions. Pat said that he would text me regularly to give me updates and that he always made sure that the kids ate vegetables when they were on the trip. I looked into his eyes and asked him to take great care of my son. They left and the kids barely looked back as they were so thrilled to get started on their adventure.

MacKenzie and Erin stayed sleeping until the normal time for them to get up that day. Regretfully, we did not wake them to say goodbye before Connor left that morning. They had their own busy activities to start the week, so we took the practical approach that morning and let them sleep in. It never crossed my mind that this would be the last chance for my daughters to say goodbye to their brother, an agony I would feel for a very long time.

Work that day was fairly normal except for two things. They were to arrive in Sedona around 8:30 a.m., and I was uncomfortable until the time that I received Pat's text that all was well. I got a text and photo from Pat around 9:00 a.m. that showed Connor and Connor very happily at the airport restaurant enjoying their meals. From that time on my discomfort lessened. I figured I was just overly worrying, and they had arrived safely so everything was okay. I spoke with my co-worker, Jessica, as we were getting our coffee. She asked about the kids, and I told her about Connor's cool and unexpected trip. I shared that he was on it as we spoke, and they had just arrived in Sedona to enjoy breakfast and the early morning sunshine at the small and quaint airport restaurant. Jessica had three boys and commented about how wonderful of an opportunity that was and that she could appreciate how excited Connor would be to go. She said she wished her boys could do something like that.

Monday proceeded as usual with family and work activities. Pat texted a few times as he promised he would and all looked great. Tuesday proceeded similarly with periodic updates and photos. Pat sent a funny photo of Connor eating vegetables in a restaurant just as he had promised. Tuesday night was special because I spoke with Connor for a short time on the phone. We had not bought Connor an iPhone yet, so he was not able to just send me a photo. He had his iPod touch separate from a simple cell phone, much to his dismay at the time, plus a separate camera.

I was very excited to talk with Connor Tuesday night because it felt like he had been gone for many nights already. I always wanted to hear from my children when they were away and learn about all of the adventures they were having. Connor acted like a normal 14-year-old boy that evening. He was happy to chat with his mom, but he was much happier being in the moment in the place that he was. They had gone to see the new release of Spiderman and were goofing around back at the room and in the pool at Sky Ranch Lodge where they were staying. He spoke with me in the distracted way that teenagers do when there is something else good happening around them. In hindsight, I am so grateful I got even those few moments. I never knew that would be the last time I would ever hear the sweet sound of my son's beautiful voice.

Wednesday came and went with additional photos of the fun they were having. They did the types of outdoors activities that most teenaged boys would love. They went to a shooting range that Connor was very excited about since it was his first time. They took a Pink Jeep tour opting for the hardest backcountry course, and they looked like they had a ball. They took a long backcountry hike, and they ate and ate. They got to choose what they wanted to eat, as much of it as they wanted, and when they wanted to eat. And always it was in the picturesque landscape of Sedona's breathtaking mountains. Pat sent a great picture of Connor and Connor eating huge ice cream cones in the middle of the day. What was extra special was that I could see in the photos that Pat was taking very good care of my son. It was not just that he spent money on him and treated him to good things. In the photo of the Pink Jeep tour, he had his arm around my Connor's waist in the same way that he had his arm around his son. When I looked at the detail in the photo at the shooting range, Pat had made sure that Connor was wearing safety glasses and earplugs. One of those photos showed Pat instructing Connor on the exact arm position for shooting. I could see he was caringly placing Connor's arms correctly and treating Connor with respect and tenderness. I was later so very appreciative of these photos. There weren't many. Pat had sent nine photos over the course of the four days, Connor's last days. But they told me my son was doing well and was really enjoying himself. Between this comfort and the passing of the days since my worries Monday morning, I relaxed a little. My life with work and family was happily usual and full.

CHAPTER 2

During

Thursday, July 26, 2012, is a day that changed the entirety of my life and being. It's almost impossible to adequately put this into words. I could never have anticipated or imagined the change that would occur on almost every level of my existence. The irony is that I awoke on Thursday like it was any other day. I was ashamed of that for the longest time. Somehow, as Connor's mother, I should have awoken with searing chest pains or a huge foreboding or SOMETHING that was going to mark this day that would become so life changing for all of us. But I didn't. I had grown more comfortable with the trip after speaking with Connor Tuesday night and seeing Pat's texts and photos over the week showing they were safe and happy. Thursday was a very busy morning with an early work meeting that I was not entirely prepared for, two daughters who had their activities to get to, and some evening activities in Connor's schedule when he returned. Preoccupied with the normal requirements of everyday life, I got ready in the early morning, hustled to get to work, and hoped to catch a few extra moments to prepare for my meeting. I texted MacKenzie and Erin when they got up to help them get organized for their day.

I received a text from Pat 11 minutes before what would later be determined as the time of the airplane crash. It was just a simple text that said, "ready for takeoff." I was leaving the office right then for my meeting, so I took note of it and thought about how happy I would be to see Connor again so soon and how happy I was that he had such a great adventure. I texted back to Pat, "what's your ETA?" I never received an answer to that text. I was not immediately concerned about that because I knew he was flying and he would not be texting while he was readying to take off. I went to my meeting and the subsequent ones right after, then found myself back at the office a little before lunch. The crash had occurred by this time, but we did not know it. I reflected later that the earth should have shaken, or I should have fainted, or something significant should have taken place at the moment of the crash because as mothers we are so deeply connected by heart and soul to our children. But this did not happen like in the movies. I would not know that it had happened for many hours to come, and after that I would remain in a huge place of shock, denial, and complete numbness for a long time.

Over lunch I was talking with my co-worker, Sunitha. She and her husband worked at our technology company, and each of our families had three children near the same ages. We had a lot of common experiences and concerns that we enjoyed sharing. At one point I joked fondly about the challenges to come with having three teenagers at the same time and how I would need to stock up on a lot of wine to stay sane throughout those years. She laughed and whole-heartily agreed. I also talked about Connor getting nearer to taking driver's education and that he would be driving on his own before I knew it. I told her a funny story that happened the week before when I was driving with Connor. Whenever I would approach a yellow light that required me to stop fast, Connor would joke and say, "Oh, Mom, you could have made that one." I would joke back and say, "Connor, that just set your driver's education class back another six weeks!" These were such incredible comments to reflect back on later because my son had already died but I had no idea.

As lunch passed and early afternoon came, I was getting increasingly uncomfortable. I couldn't even begin to form words around my discomfort, not even to myself. But inside a tsunami was beginning to form, and I was having difficulty knowing where to turn or what to do. My soul knew something, but I could not possibly allow anything to surface on a conscious level. The horror was just too much to allow my heart or soul to consider. By that time, I had been texting Pat and Connor periodically to get a sense of when they would be back. I thought that Pat had said they would leave after breakfast, but I wasn't sure I recalled that correctly, and he had left it open and flexible for them to depart when they felt ready. I thought that Pat may not have texted back because maybe there is a lot to do with flying a plane home and getting everything taken care of to complete an airplane trip. Then they had to get the car and drive back from the airport. Since the return time was open ended, I thought they may have left a little later and decided to stop for lunch before they returned home. Our Connor loved to fly and Pat knew this, so I thought Pat may have taken extra time to show Connor scenic things on the way back thereby taking longer to return. I did not know it at the time, but I was already experiencing a panic attack inside because of my terror and the uncertainty as well as my inner knowing.

When I texted Connor, at first it was casual. "Hi love, can't wait to see you when you get home. So glad you had a great time." Later, "Do you have any idea when you will get back home?" Later, "Please let me know what the plan is, I haven't heard from you in a while." Then later, my desperation and panic were starting to seep through. I sent him a series of texts telling him all of the plans for the evening and the next few days. There was no logical reason for this. Maybe this was my desperate attempt at doing something to stop the fire and panic that was rising inside me. Somehow if Connor had his itinerary, and I had spelled it out to him and the Universe by putting it in the physical form of texts, surely nothing out of the ordinary could be happening. He had evening soccer practice upon his return, and I reminded him that he would be able to wear his brand new soccer shoes that we had just purchased before the trip because he had grown so much again and needed new ones for the season.

Erin was spending this particular week at a horse camp that was about 30 minutes north in Placitas, New Mexico. At 11, she had been a horse lover for many years, and this was the week of a lifetime for her as well. I dropped her off in the morning before work and picked her up at the end of the day after work. She had always been a horse lover and wanted to learn how to ride one when we moved to New Mexico from the Midwest five years earlier. She had a fabulous time each day learning how to care for the horses, ride them, groom them, feed and water them, and exercise them. I was happy to pick her up every day and see her shining face at peace from being in such a special space and doing what she loved. MacKenzie had turned 16 just six weeks earlier, and she was working at her first job at a child care center for at-risk children. I felt very happy that week knowing that all three of my kids were enjoying a week of summer break doing what they loved and what helped them to thrive and grow.

It was time for me to leave work and drive to pick up Erin. I left very anxious and in a panic that I was desperately trying to suppress. I was driving to get Erin from camp just like I had done the previous three days. I was running late because I had started to text Pat's wife, Trish, before I left in order to get answers while trying to choke down the panic that was getting intense and overwhelming. I did not hear back from Trish. I learned later that I only had her home phone number in my cell phone and was trying to text that number. I did not realize this was the home number and not her cell number since I was already so scared, and it was marked incorrectly in my phone. I was not aware that Trish had been driving back from Colorado Springs at the time I was trying to call her home number.

The drive through Placitas about 20 minutes later was so odd. After turning off I25 and heading east, I encountered a bad rainstorm. These often begin out-of-the-blue in New Mexico and can be a deluge for just five or ten minutes. At that same time, my co-worker, Nora, had called me from New York City where she was working for a few days and visiting a friend. Nora and I were close, and we were talking about a work issue that seemed very important. I was not very present for the conversation. My body was beginning to break, and I was beginning to understand deep in my soul, if not yet in my mind, what was happening. I was like a robot talking about whatever the work things were so that I did not have to face the immense fear that had risen in me. As the rainstorm pounded on my windshield, and in the middle of a sentence with Nora, I just knew. I did not know what happened, but I knew a catastrophe had happened and felt it in the depths of my being. I interrupted Nora without explanation and made an excuse that I had to get off the phone immediately to be safe in the heavy downpour. I could barely concentrate on driving.

Once I arrived at the horse camp, my panic eased up a little. I still massively felt the foreboding, but my daughter's beautiful, bright face distracted and somewhat stabilized me. She had so much to show me about her day. I felt terrible, but I rushed her through it because I felt I had to get home and see Connor to rid these horrid feelings that were swimming inside of me. I had to get home fast to yell at him and Pat for giving me this scare. Erin quickly showed me which horses she had taken care of that day pointing them out by name and the unique details about each. She showed me where they had ridden and the hardest jobs they had to do. Then we quickly departed.

I drove home, and I felt slightly more relaxed as Erin's innocence brought back a little beauty while she told me stories of her day. The glow on her was so wonderful that it was the medicine that allowed me to drive a car when the panic still raged deep inside of me. When I was about five minutes from our home, I was making the turn off of San Mateo Road and turning east onto Academy Road toward our house. My cell phone rang. For safety reasons I never answered the cell phone while driving. If it was in the back near Erin, she would sometimes look to see who it was and answer it. It was Bryan so she answered it and was ready to tell him about her day.

I did not hear what Bryan said, but I could tell from Erin's response that he screamed into the phone for her to give it to me. She said I was driving and could not talk, but he must have yelled strongly enough because she told me I had to answer it now. I will never forget the words I heard while making that turn. He said, "We just read on Facebook that Connor died in a plane crash." They were the most horrid and incomprehensible words I could have ever heard. So horrid that I could not take them in. I tried not to run off the road as my body was spasming and shaking beyond belief. I could barely breathe. I said "WHAT?" I asked who, what, why about this ridiculous statement he had just said. He said one of the students from Connor's class had posted on Facebook, "Connor P. and Connor M. died in a plane crash today." I could not begin to fathom what to do, and I was still trying to drive my little girl home safely in rush hour traffic. After I hung up, the student's family was called, and the posting was immediately removed. I was panicked, and my mind just could not believe it, although my soul was already in the early stages of agony. I just tried to keep my eyes focused on the wheel to complete the remaining five-minute drive home.

I ran with Erin into the house, and MacKenzie and Bryan were screaming and crying. I had never heard such painful sounds from either of them. It crushed my heart and knocked all breath from me to hear it. I had experienced many serious challenges in my life and was a good problem-solver with even the toughest of situations. This was what I knew and was my strength. I had no capability at that point to believe this horrific possibility that my son had died nor was I able to open myself to that awaiting anguish. I spent the next couple of hours in a masked and seemingly calm problem-solving mode pleading with everyone to stop panicking and to just work with me to figure out what was happening. There HAD to be another explanation other than this. After all, there was no proof except a stupid Facebook posting, and that it was 4 p.m., and my son was not home, and I had not heard from him, Trish, or Pat. But still, I could not go there. It was impossible.

The movies show us how it is supposed to work. Someone comes to the house, or someone makes that awful phone call. No one came to our house. No one called us. How on earth could my beautiful son be dead? It just didn't work that way. So I proceeded with my best-ever problem-solving skills to correct this thing. I had no adequate phone numbers to call. I googled, I guessed, I looked in an old phone book. I always collected this emergency information and in all these years of parenting had never needed to use it. Why didn't I have anything now when I desperately needed it? I tried calling the Albuquerque private airport. I tried calling the Sedona airport. I tried calling the Albuquerque police. I tried calling the Sedona police. Each one took quite some time just to find the correct number and then to get through. And no one could tell me anything. I tried calling Trish again. I tried calling Connor again. I tried calling Pat again. We did not know at the time that nobody had officially notified Trish yet either, but a reporter had contacted her and told her the suspected news. She was desperately trying to return to Albuquerque from Colorado.

I looked in the school directory and called one of the fathers whose son was a close friend of Connor Porter's, and I was able to speak with him. He was not able to tell me anything. I screamed into the phone in a mother's direst plea. "Please tell me something, I can't get ahold of anybody. People are telling me my son died, and I can't get anyone to give me any information on whether it is true. Please, please help me." I can only imagine how painful that phone call was for this nice man. He did not know what to do. No one knew why someone had not told us yet.

It wasn't until fully into the next day that we learned why no one had come and no one had called. The police cannot contact the family of a person who died until the person has been fully identified. This was impossible to do because of the horrific crash. No one could reach out to us with an official notification. This was a horrible glitch in the system and caused extensive and unnecessary agony to us and everyone involved.

Word of this tragedy traveled very fast in our community through texts and messaging. Somehow while my family was wandering around the house crying in pain and in the dark, and I was frozen in denial calling anyone possible, loving people in our community were figuring out what to do and how to help. I broke down and made a call to my sister, Laurie, in Milwaukee. How painful that call must have been for her. I did not know what to do. I was unable to think at all, I was in complete shock, and I was just trying to keep breathing. The words were so painful that I could only speak tentatively and in barely a whisper to her. All I could utter was, "I think my son might have just died in a plane crash." That was all I had.

The rest of the day felt and still feels like a rushing river just swirling over us and tossing us this way and that way without end. At one point, I recall sitting down at our home computer and googling plane crashes in Arizona that day. I was trying to find any news story that might tell me whether my son had died. I couldn't actually function. I was in a state akin to a constant panic attack but did not know it. I could not focus my eyes on the keyboard, and my brain could not complete the processes of translating what I wanted to do into pressing the appropriate keys. My hands were shaking so hard I could hardly still them. I was hyperventilating, so I could not really breathe or speak. I was not crying yet, because if I cried, it was real, and Connor might be dead. And with no proof of that yet, I had to hold out hope.

Heather, the mother of one of MacKenzie's friends, had arrived and gently asked me what I was doing. I could barely speak, but I whispered to her, "Everyone is telling me that my son died in a plane crash. But that's impossible. Because no one has come to tell us. No one has called us, and no one has come to our door. They always do that when someone dies. So I think he really didn't. And I don't know why everyone keeps saying that, so I am trying to find a news story that will tell me whether Connor died today." She asked me if I was finding what I needed, and I cried a little and told her "no." I said that I could not figure out what to do, and I could not press the right keys, and I was getting very frustrated that I couldn't do this important task. She suggested that maybe I stop and I said "no." She asked if I wanted help and I told her "yes." I asked her to sit down and find it for me. I got up and left and asked her to call me when she knew something.

When I went back to the main area of the house, I could not fathom that it was my house or what was happening. I couldn't find any air and decided that I needed to try and breathe. I went outside with my dog, probably with the intent to take a walk. If I walked this would all go away once I could breathe and come back to the house. I only got two houses down when I couldn't move my limbs any further since I was in shock but did not realize it. Every limb in my body felt like cement. So I laid down on my side in the fetal position with my cheek against the pavement. Somehow feeling my cheek on the pavement made me feel alive, and I could not feel any life inside my body otherwise. My gentle dog sat straight up in front of my head, guarding me with her life from anything that came near me. Heather must have followed me, and she came over and asked if I wanted to stay there. Asia growled hard at her. Asia never growled at people. She was a rescue dog and was too afraid. But she knew something was terribly wrong with me, and she was protecting the me that was barely alive. I told Heather I wanted to stay there, and she walked a little of the way back while keeping me in sight.

Nothing felt right. Nothing I could do or anywhere that I could go felt remotely right because my world as I knew it had just ended. I did not stay on the pavement long. I was immobilized and antsy at the same time. I just wanted every horrible feeling and pain inside of me to leave but could not figure out what to do with myself to possibly make that happen. I went back toward my house for lack of knowing what else to do. As I arrived at the house, I noticed there were numerous cars out front and people coming into our house. These were all lovely "angels" who would be the miracle workers that helped us make it through the days, weeks, months, and years to come. But at that moment I hated them. How could they come? People only come like that for one reason. Because someone died. They couldn't come. How dare they do that? If they were there, Connor might actually have died. I wanted to scream at them to go home. They couldn't be doing this. It might make Connor die if this was what was really happening. If it did not happen, then maybe he had not died. These desperate thoughts ran back and forth and swam around and around in my mind.

I was powerless over everything and my world was spinning. All I wanted was to stop what was happening, but there was nothing I could do. There was nothing I could do to change the one thing that was more crucial than anything I had ever wanted to change in my life. Everything kept going. People came and went. People stayed and didn't stay. I didn't know. And I don't remember now. It was like an out-of-body experience where I was watching a really, really bad horror movie. I remember asking anyone who I saw whether we should go to Sedona. I didn't know what to do. I guess somewhere inside of me I knew that

Connor was gone, but the conscious part of me felt like if I went there, then maybe I could fix it and save him. People told us it was probably better to stay here because there would not be much we could do, and Connor would likely no longer be in Sedona. I didn't know what to do with that. I am a mother and my child was not with me. I felt I needed to go to him, but we did not even know where he was at that time. And we needed to take care of our daughters who were in more pain that I could ever bear to see.

I remember many people helping with MacKenzie and Erin, for which I was extremely grateful. I was having trouble breathing or focusing on anything, and my ability at that time to help them was feeble. I remember laying down next to Bryan after it had gotten very late and all the visitors had left. I just laid there and could not figure out what to do. How does a mother just close out the day and go to sleep with one less child? It's impossible, immoral, and wrong from every breath and cell of her being. And somehow, if I went to sleep without Connor here and woke up tomorrow, Connor might really be dead. I still could not possibly accept this truth and would look for any reason to not face the horror. And how could a mother sleep if her child was missing and even remotely possibly dead?

I awoke in the morning after a few hours of fitful sleep. My waking was the strangest imaginable. When I first woke up, I felt a really odd feeling but I could not identify what it was. And then just a moment later, it all came flooding back to me, knocking me over and taking my breath away. This is a pattern that would repeat itself every morning for many, many months to come. I did not know where to turn or how to make it stop. I could not run from this thing, but that is the only thing I wanted to do.

I got up in a dark house, and the only thing I could think to do was call my sister. I had no idea what time it was. Except for Bryan's parents, my whole family was back in Milwaukee, and I knew I needed help to even take the next step. I talked to Laurie for a short time and learned that my immediate family members were trying to figure out how and when each would get to Albuquerque. My Dad and his wife lived in Arizona, but they were in Milwaukee visiting at that time and staying with my sister, Cathy. In the meantime, my Uncle Bill was able to fly out quickly, and he arrived by the next morning.

Trish came over in the morning with a friend and her brother, who had flown in from out of state. She told us that she had found out through a reporter and not an official source either because there was no confirmation of the passengers yet. She let us know the little she could confirm, but still there was no information from any official source or any details. The reporter had described the unique plane colors to her, though, and from this she was sure. Pat had loved the color purple, and the wing of the plane in the crash had this distinct purple. Although I did not want to, I could see in their eyes that this nightmare was real, even when the only thing I wanted to hear was that this was a cruel joke. Everyone was in shock, and we could do nothing more than shed tears and mutter disbelief while being half frozen.

Through the course of the day things just happened. I received an email from Connor's soccer team providing details about the game that night and a change in the schedule. How could they not know? Who tells them? Do I respond to the email and say my son was missing and might be dead? Then shortly afterward someone must have told someone else on the team because I read another team email telling the team about Connor's death. How surreal that was for me to read the announcement to his team about my hell. I was still at the computer periodically because I was looking for any information or news that I could find about the crash, and people were sending supportive messages as well that I desperately needed.

In the late afternoon on Friday, I received a phone call from the Sedona police department. The officer said he could not tell me anything or confirm anything but they "believed my son might have been involved in a plane crash." It was another crazy thing for me to hear on top of all of the things I had heard in the previous 24 hours that I couldn't comprehend. Then they told me they needed me to send Connor's dental records. It felt like a blow to my stomach with enough strength to double me over. How does a mother survive getting asked to send her son's dental records to the police station for identification? Somehow, I located the number for our kind pediatric dentist who had known our three children since we moved to Albuquerque. He has three sons of his own, and I worked to find the words to ask him to do this. I do not know where the words came from, and I do not know how he survived the pain of that call. But I heard the breath knocked from him when I said the words as it had been knocked from me when I heard them. He could not find any words except "okay."

A vigil in the park was arranged for later that evening by the parents on Connor's soccer team. This was all so new that I didn't really understand what a vigil exactly was and had to ask about this. It was so beautiful but so horrible and awful all at the same time. Why were we having this? What was I supposed to do? It hurt beyond any wound I had ever felt in my life. I just wanted everything to end so this pain would stop.

Finally, 48 hours later on Saturday afternoon, we received the knock on the door from the Albuquerque police. They felt horrible about the delay and explained the series of policies that prevented anyone from coming sooner. By this time, it did not really matter. It mattered only it that it was another assault on top of all the previous ones. But it did not matter because Connor was gone.

Saturday we had to go to French's Funeral Home to talk about arrangements. This was another blow to my gut that doubled me over. I absolutely did not want to do it and said "no." I figured if I just did not go, I might not have to do this. But like everything else to come, someone gently pushed us along to take care of it. My Uncle Bill physically helped us outside and put Bryan and me into the car. Others had arrived to stay with MacKenzie and Erin, and we were off to discuss urns, services, visitations, and more things that I did not want to know anything about. And with each anguishing word, I could feel a further and further ripping of my heart.

Later I had calls from the funeral home in Prescott, Arizona, which is where they were transferred because Sedona is very small. The funeral home was calling about the death certificate. I needed to proofread the death certificate and sign off on it so they could release the body. Now my son was a body. When I received the certificate, I had to read horrible words in the description of what happened to our beautiful Connor. I could not comprehend why my wonderful life was all of a sudden like this and instantly full of such enormous pain. How could those words be associated with my son, Connor?

That afternoon we received a visit from the Minister of our church. All I wanted from her was answers. Tell me this is impossible. Tell me how this can happen. Tell me what we do now. Tell me if there is a God. Tell me how can there be a God when this happens. I asked her to tell me whether she thought there was a God when a child as innocent as Connor is horribly killed at 14. I asked her what we were supposed to do to survive. She provided comfort as best she could, but she did not have many answers to give and was in great pain herself.

The following days were filled with endless dark tasks that I did not want to do, and every one of them was horrible. My sister, Cathy, took me to the bank to sign the papers establishing a memorial fund in Connor's name for the many people who asked where they could contribute. Other friends helped us write an obituary. I was asked to create a list of people to call to inform them of Connor's death. We asked our friend, Sylvia, to be our spokesperson at a press conference with the media because I could not breathe much less speak publicly.

MacKenzie, Erin, and I needed to find dresses and shoes that were appropriate to wear for Connor's memorial service. How were we to do such a task? We planned a memorial service in Albuquerque that would be held one week after the accident. We also planned a second service in Milwaukee the following week because we had an entire life there before we moved to Albuquerque five short years before. We still had most of our family there and many, many close friends who would want to attend Connor's memorial service. It just went on and on. The decisions and tasks seemed to never end.

Many people came over during the next few days, which was lifesaving to us. So many people helped us that I can hardly believe it when I reflect back. In addition to meals and helping with arrangements, friends assisted in so many other ways, too. They helped feed all of the people who were there assisting, cleaned our floors, cleaned our bathrooms, tried to soothe us whenever possible, and attempted to make sure we ate and drank something. We did not ask for any of these things, but people just acted from their hearts as they wanted to do anything to help. Many of MacKenzie's and Erin's friends came over to be with her and Erin, for which I was again grateful. I recall walking down the hallway that contained our three children's bedrooms and their bathroom. There must have been about 10 teenagers in that bathroom at that moment. Being a double bathroom, it was a bit larger, but it was not that big. There were teenagers everywhere including MacKenzie's friend, Chris, who was about 6'4" and sitting in the bathtub. When I asked why they were all congregated there, they said they wanted space away from everyone else in the house, but that they all needed to be close together. And that was the space that fit the best. We all shared a small smile of warmth at that moment, and it was a tiny bright spot that each of us needed amidst the pain.

We held Connor's Albuquerque memorial service the following Thursday. I was very grateful for the many people who assisted to make this happen. Planning a memorial service for anyone is a hard task, but planning one for your 14-year-old child is unbearable. On the one hand, I didn't want to have a service at all and go through more searing and public pain. On the other hand, Connor was an amazing human being, and I wanted to be able to tell anyone who would listen about who he was, what made him so special, how he impacted this world during his short life, and what he meant to so many. Together we all set about the task of creating a lovely and meaningful recognition of Connor's life as best we could.

The day of the service was beyond what I thought my heart could take. Our family and close friends were driven in large cars from our house to the church. When we arrived, we were taken to a side entrance so we could have privacy with our extended family in the back room before the service began. As we drove up I felt like I was having a heart attack. Although my head knew why we were there, when I saw the throngs of people who were gathered to say goodbye to my precious child, it was almost impossible to take. I was shocked at the number of people I saw. There were too many to fit inside our church, and people were just scattered everywhere on the grounds and in the nearby buildings on the property. I later learned there were approximately 650 people there. And that did not include most of my family and many of our friends who were in Milwaukee waiting for the service we would hold there the following week, which another 300 people attended. I remember spotting various people here and there from all different aspects of our lives. It was lovely but also confusing to see all of these people from different parts of our life together in one place when I was in the most pain of my life. It was difficult for the many people waiting outside because the temperature at the end of July in Albuquerque is very hot. Many people waited in suits and dresses through that uncomfortable heat to join in supporting us. The church placed TVs in various locations around the grounds so that all of the people attending could be a part of the service when there wasn't enough room to house everyone inside the church.

The most difficult moment for me was when we were led from the private side room into the main church area where everyone had already been seated. I walked in, and for the first time I truly understood that this service was the public honoring of Connor's life and the formal recognition marking the end of his life. It was crushing, and I almost fainted walking in. The finality of it overwhelmed me. And I was in pain beyond description.

The service was as beautiful as a service for your child could be. Every person who assisted with it, whether speaking or helping with arrangements, made the day a great honoring of the beautiful person that Connor was and the meaningful life he led. I was so proud of MacKenzie and Erin who each wrote and spoke beautiful words about their love for and relationship with their brother. Michael, who had been our children's piano teacher the five years we had been in Albuquerque, played piano at the service. Michael played pieces of Connor's original compositions, which were beautiful. Reverend Christine Robinson spoke as many loving words of wisdom as she could find to our family and to all the broken-hearted who were there.

The line to speak with us after the service was longer than I had ever seen. This was a testament to the amount of love people had for Connor and our family and the gracious support they were willing to give us. Greeting bereaved parents after a service for their child is a very humbling and painful task. I appreciated all who waited a very long time in a hot and sweaty line to do so. Albuquerque is quite diverse religiously and spiritually. One of the beautiful gifts from that long line were the condolences, prayers, and blessings offered by so many people who held different faith and spiritual traditions. People greeted us with the most honoring words from their individual faiths, and we learned that

Connor and our family were being prayed for in many diverse ways. I did not know exactly what to do with this experience but it touched me.

Despite finding desperately-needed moments of beauty, those minutes, hours, and days were agony. I don't remember the details of what followed that day or many of the others to come. My heart had taken more than I ever thought it could bear. All I knew was that I could not believe this was my life now, and I had no idea how to begin to live it.

CHAPTER 3

After

PHYSICALLY

Somehow, I had made it through the horrors of the first two weeks, and I felt like I had lived a year already. I had no idea how on earth I would be able to make it another week much less a month, a year, or many years. It felt completely impossible and hopelessly cruel.

The days and months that followed continued to batter my family and me regularly. There was the first of everything. Pain after pain piled one on top of another. There was the pain within our family as each person's path of grieving was different than that of the others. This could separate us despite our best efforts to move forward together with this new, smaller family of four. I had terrible worry and fear while trying to carve a healthy path forward for my devastated daughters. Feelings of being a moving body with nothing left inside consumed my days. The guilt, regret, and despair I experienced were suffocating.

To add on cruelty, the rest of life went on. During this first year, I had to pay bills, function the best I could at work, do laundry, and deal with jerky people on the phone who were taking out their crappy days on me. I had to walk around in the grocery story looking like I was normal when I was anything but. I accidentally bumped into people who commented that I shouldn't be so rude, but they did not know that I couldn't focus for even small periods of time. I forgot to say please, thank you, or provide a complete response at times because things just did not register in my brain the same now. So much space in my head and heart was occupied by this new pain. I often could not speak much at all because I didn't have words to describe all that was happening inside of me or the chaos that surrounded me.

I sort of wanted to wear a big sign around my neck that said, "Please excuse me, my son was just killed in a plane crash, and I can't function." This way I would not have to explain to anyone why I looked like the wind would knock me over at any moment, why I looked so confused, why I could not count change in my purse, and why I could not answer an easy question. We rode the waves of these brutal encounters one day to the next without reprieve, and I am not sure how we ever made it through these painful experiences that seemed to just never end.

The one-year anniversary passed, and I fell into a new black hole that I could not comprehend. We had "made it through" all of those terribly agonizing firsts without our son. We had "arrived" somewhere because it was the one-year mark, but where? Why didn't I feel any less pain? Why didn't I feel any better? How come I didn't have any better idea of how to live the second year without my son much less the next 40 or 50? While there were many books about how to survive the first year, there were not as many to tell a grieving mother how she could survive so many more years when she felt depleted and the people and resources around her were far fewer. I was beginning to feel that the next stage of this journey was a more internal one, for which I felt completely ill-equipped and at a loss for where to begin.

SPIRITUALLY

"We do not receive wisdom; we must discover it for ourselves after a journey through the wilderness that no one else can make."
~ Marcel Proust

Double Rainbow Sedona, AZ,
Airport Crash Site; July 27, 2012

Before we lost Connor, I considered myself to be a spiritual person. I had experienced different religious and spiritual paths throughout my life that helped me better understand our greater existence here. I was raised Catholic for my very early years of childhood, and during my adult years I spent time in Buddhism, agnosticism, and atheism. We joined the Unitarian Universalist Faith when our children were born and were very active church members both in Milwaukee and Albuquerque for many years after. Each of these paths I followed fit the experiences of my life at those times. Together they created more of a deep and expansive spiritual path for me and less of a singular religious one. After I had my first child and knew the incredible wonders and miracles of that experience, I believed in my heart there must be a greater Source that created all that is around us. I did not have all the answers on what existed after we died or whether there was a Heaven in the way people described. But I never believed in a punishing God or one that sent people to Hell because they believed something different. I believed we were all born in the Divine's image. In the years before the airplane crash, I did not focus extensively on these things because I was busy enjoying the beauty and joy of raising my full, young family.

Suddenly questions of what comes after this life, whether there is a Heaven, who gets to go there and why, and many more, became of imperative concern for me. I could not fathom that a person whose soul was as big and pure as Connor's was just gone now and no longer existed. This did not make any sense to me. I was haunted by this question as I navigated each of the painful experiences and moments of that first year. I did not realize it at the time because I was too frozen and numb, but little by little I was learning new perspectives about these questions as I began to receive signs from Connor that took me quite some time to recognize, believe, understand, and trust.

Immediately after Connor's memorial service, I started to devour books written by parents who had lost children. I needed to feel like less of an alien knowing that this experience had happened to other good people, too. I scoured the books for any grain of hope they could provide. I felt so powerless and desolate that if an entire book rendered one sentence of hope or one helpful perspective, it felt like I had been given a gift of gold.

In many of these books, parents described their experiences of receiving signs from their children. I desperately wanted to believe this could be true, but I had not experienced signs from anyone previously in my life who had passed away. I didn't know whether this could be true or was an attempt at grasping for hope. As I look back, many signs came to me early on before I could recognize them as such. It took time for me to find a place in my heart and mind that could make sense of them and understand that this was what I was experiencing.

One of the first signs that was tremendously impactful for me and made me ask bigger questions happened about four weeks after the accident. I had been driving home from somewhere, and I wasn't paying attention. I was still in shock and quite numb. Normally I never had my phone near me when I drove, and I was vehement about not texting while driving. But those weeks after the accident were a fog. I did not feel like I was inside my body, yet I had to function in life and this included driving. On this particular day, I had not noticed that I had my phone in my hand. I was driving in the left-most lane of a three-lane street, and without knowing it I was going about 15 miles over the speed limit of 40 MPH. I didn't realize that I was accelerating and texting. I had not seen that a white car pulled out from a parking lot off the right side of the road without sufficient space to cross the three lanes before I reached it. I was looking down at my phone and suddenly heard a booming voice say "LOOK UP!" At that second I looked up, slammed on my brakes, and I just missed hitting the driver at that excessive speed. As my heart pounded and I realized what had occurred, I looked to find the source of the "voice." I knew it was in my head, but I could not comprehend what had happened. There was no radio on, no phone noise, no window open, no one in my car, and no one anywhere near. I pulled into the nearest parking lot as quickly as I could and just stopped for a moment. My head was spinning and there were tears running down my cheeks. I realized that wherever that message came from, whether it was Divine guidance, Connor, inner wisdom, whatever it was…a true miracle had just occurred.

Following this occurrence, a beautiful and curious experience happened on my first day back at work. My employers had graciously extended a leave of absence to me as I plodded through the earliest weeks of this horror. At eight weeks I had to return to work, and I felt like I did not belong in my body.

My co-workers were wonderful and tried to extend any support they could. They let me lead the way that first day in terms of how quickly and deeply I wanted to move into things. Even with this gentle start, within about one hour I found myself sobbing at my desk. I concluded at that moment that tears at work would probably be something I could not control and decided I would permit myself to go outside and sit when they came. Unless I allowed myself that, I knew there was no possibility I would make it through any meetings much less a full day.

As I sat quietly outside, I wept and thought a lot. My thoughts were random and all over the place. At eight weeks there is not yet a moment when you can think of anything without remembering that your child died. As I sat on the ground, I was pondering Connor's young life. For some reason the specific thought came into my head that maybe Connor had to leave while he was still young and innocent. He had not had any problems with common teenage challenges like drugs, alcohol, or behavioral problems. Given Connor's nature I did not think those things would have become problems later, but maybe he needed to leave here before he was old enough for those things to possibly become issues. At that very moment the most beautiful small, pure, white feather came trickling down in front of my face. It did not come straight down but rather waved back and forth in front of me very slowly on its descent. My heart warmed when I saw this because of the specific timing it happened. I immediately looked up to find out where it came from. To my surprise, I could not identify any place it could have come from. There were no trees or birds near, no nests anywhere, and no breeze. No animals and no other people. It was just me there. I had new tears in my eyes, but I did not have words to explain them. Although I did not understand or trust that signs from my child who died could be real at that time, I knew that something beyond me and what I could fully understand or explain had just happened. I had a tiny flutter of hope that I desperately needed and love flooded from my heart. Afterward, I more easily returned inside to face what was ahead of me.

This small moment gave me so much peace and comfort that I wanted to replicate it again. Of course I could not do that as I just waited and wondered if another sign would come. But my urgency for more made me ponder things that had happened earlier, which at the time felt unusual but did not fully register as perhaps something special.

In the week following the accident, a parent at our school who was a news reporter named Joseph asked if he could do a story about Connor. His son knew Connor, and Joseph wanted to honor Connor's beautiful life rather than focus on his tragic death. I said that was a lovely idea as long as I did not have to be in it. I had panic attacks frequently, and I surely did not want to appear on television when I was struggling to find any words to describe my loss. Joseph let me know that the story would only be meaningful if Bryan and I told it as his parents. In honor of Connor I agreed because I felt the world should know about the amazing son we loved so much.

Joseph was wonderfully respectful and took images of our family and our home. When he sat down to interview Bryan and me, the strangest thing happened. As soon as Joseph asked me the first question, I began to have a panic attack and could not find any words. Seconds later, however, I felt this amazing lifting up of my spirit and warmth flooding my body. All of a sudden my heart did not hurt, and I was filled with only beautiful, loving feelings. I was able to speak joyfully and calmly about the beautiful person Connor was and the amazing things he brought to this world. It felt wonderful, and I was glad to feel that way even if I could not explain how or why it was happening. I felt like I was inside another person's body because I did not feel any pain and everything felt peaceful and serene for just that short time during the interview. When I saw the newscast later, it was as if I was watching someone else. I had no idea how this was possible with the pain that I had in my body, which returned after we finished the interview. I did not realize it at the time, but Connor had truly lifted me up so that I could do what was so important to me in that moment. I was very grateful, and it is a feeling that I can still feel today that is very sacred to me.

As I work with people who have lost a loved one, an important topic we discuss is the signs they may receive from their loved one. When we attended our local support group meetings with The Compassionate Friends or The Children's Grief Center, some of the bereaved parents had experienced many signs from their child who had died, a few had wondered whether they had experienced a sign, and others had not experienced any at all. Irrespective of religious belief or nonbelief, the people who had experienced and recognized signs felt a stronger and continuing connection with their child, which aided feelings of hope and healing amidst the pain.

One woman who had lost her son experienced a wonderful healing moment when he showed her a sign she could not disregard. Her son always had a bad habit of leaving his bedroom ceiling fan on when he left the house. This was a habit that drove his mom crazy. After he had passed, she started noticing that the fan in his bedroom would be on when no one in the house had turned it on. At the beginning, she just figured another person in the family had turned it on but did not remember doing so since deep grief tends to fog a person's memory. But as it kept happening repeatedly she wondered more about it. Then she noticed that whenever this happened, she had a really warm feeling in her heart that provided extra closeness to her son. Once it happened more frequently, she began to thank her son. She knew this phenomenon was impossible from a physical standpoint, and it was her son saying hello in a way she would undoubtedly recognize to give her comfort. This awakening changed her ability to move forward through her grief and pain and also increased her desire to learn more about how to recognize signs from him.

Another amazing thing happened to us a few days after the news interview when the newscast of our story began. Many of the people in town for the service were in our home, and they all gathered around in the living room to watch the story. We had a large 16"x 20" framed photo of Connor in his 8th-grade soccer team uniform from the previous fall season. It was a beautiful photo that showed his big, gregarious smile and the vibrant energy he brought to everything he did. The local photography studio that took it gave us this framed photo as a gift after the accident. We had not had a chance to hang it on the wall yet, and I had placed it next to the TV before the start of the news. Once Connor's story began, our calm dog, Asia, became anxious and went right over to the photo. She was looking at the photo and whining loudly. The whole group noticed it, and we all looked at one another baffled. Then she went up to the photo and starting pushing it side-to-side with her nose while she whined louder and looked back and forth between us and the picture. She had never acted like that before, and it was if she felt something. As soon as Connor's story finished, she stopped and quietly went and laid down again. She never did that again, and the picture remained there for quite a while. It was really an incredible moment. No one had words for what happened, but you could see on everyone's faces that we witnessed something special that no one could explain.

We continued on our journey of grief during the second year attending support group meetings and individual grief counseling. I also continued my voracious reading, always searching for anything that could answer my haunting questions or help me to feel Connor more. My experience of finding feathers kept occurring sporadically. I found them in odd places when no birds, trees, or nests were around and always when I was in deep pain and desperately needed support. Over the course of the next couple of years, both Bryan and I received feathers regularly. Whenever I would find one, I placed it in a bowl with the others, and over time I amassed quite a collection. Each and every time this happened I felt a momentary reprieve in my heart and felt Connor was somehow near me.

We also had several amazing experiences with hummingbirds. There was a lovely patio on the side of our house containing large trees and a grassy area. We never had hummingbirds in our yard before nor did we have any feeders out to encourage them into our yard. One day while sitting outside at our patio table, we saw a hummingbird flying around in front of us. It seemed like it was dancing around just for us and brought a moment of brightness to our painful day. A couple of days later when we sat outside at the table, we saw two hummingbirds fluttering around the trees and the table. This brought us another moment of peace and smiles. These two hummingbirds kept visiting and doing this daily from then on, and a couple of weeks later we noticed that they were building a nest right above the chair where I always sat. I looked up one day, and they were happily working right above my head. A few days after seeing the nest, one of the hummingbirds did the most amazing thing while I sat outside in my chair. It came right up to my face, just inches away, and stayed there flitting away while locking eyes with me. I could feel this beautiful energy and experienced a sacred moment that I could not describe. I looked at Bryan and said, "I think there is something happening here that is more than we can see." I could not explain exactly what was happening, but this surely was not a random or solely physical occurrence.

It is not unusual for bereaved parents to receive signs in the form of coins. I read about this and then heard from many who had this experience. Al had lost his 17-year-old son to suicide. Al struggled tremendously with guilt along with the despair and anger following his son's death. Al's son loved to collect things, and he had acquired a large collection of coins from various places and time periods. He was always proud to show his Dad the newest of his discoveries.

For a long time, Al could not feel his son's presence and desperately needed to know he was okay. After he and I talked about the many common ways in which parents receive signs from their children, Al wanted to experience this so that he might feel a measure of peace. I encouraged him to ask his son to send a sign that would reflect their special relationship with one another. I suggested Al slow down and observe what took place around him more, experiencing things with his heart and not just his eyes and thoughts. After a few weeks, Al received his first sign and it was a coin. He walked his dog along the same path each night and had never before seen a coin. But on this particular day, he noticed an old quarter right under his foot. When he noticed it, he felt something in his heart before he thought about it with his mind. It was the very type of coin that his son had in his collection. He was skeptical and hopeful at the same time. He asked his son to show him another sign if this was indeed him so that he could be more confident. Al discovered another coin in the same place on another walk just a few days later. After the second one, he knew this was a sign and his heart opened. He continued to thank his son for the signs and asked him to send more. Over time Al received many coins in his path, sometimes two or three of them at a time. He later began to receive feathers, too. Al was able to begin to find moments of peace that his son was okay, and he felt more hopeful about the future since he could feel his son's loving and continuing presence.

A very difficult time for me was the six-month anniversary of Connor's death. Six months took me closer to the one-year mark, and that made me feel very distant from Connor and more helpless. This feeling was intense in the week leading up to this day, and I was in great despair when I woke up. I was still very new to this and did not know how it all worked, but I asked Connor for an extra big sign to help me through the day. And I told him I would keep my heart and eyes open as best I could so I would notice it.

My heart always felt a little better when I was outside even if it was cold. I decided to take my morning coffee onto the patio with a few blankets since it was January, in an attempt to feel somewhat alive inside. When I walked outside, I was amazed at what I saw. Up to this point, I had received a single feather or perhaps two at once, but that was the most I had ever seen at a time. On the grass right next to the chair where I always sat was a scattering of feathers like I had never seen before. There were more than 50 feathers of all types, sizes, and colors. I checked to see whether a bird might have been killed or attacked nearby that would explain this. But there was nothing anywhere near. There were no birds, no nests, no remains, or anything that could explain the beautiful array of feathers. They were all so pristine and untouched that they felt very sacred. It was the most amazing and confirming gift I could have received. I cried tears mixed of pain and joy. My heart opened a little more on this extra painful day, and I felt a little peace and hope for something better to come.

A man I worked with had a similar experience with his adult son who was shockingly killed in an accident. He was having a particularly difficult day on the first anniversary of his son's passing. He did not know how he could possibly mark it or celebrate his son's life when he was still experiencing so much deep grief. While he thought he might have felt his son's presence over the past year, he could not figure out what people meant by signs as he didn't recognize having seen any. But he felt desperate, so early that morning he asked his son to send a sign that he could surely recognize. He wanted so badly to feel more connected to his son like he had heard other bereaved parents describe.

The father disliked his son's bad habit of smoking. While he had tried to convince his son to quit, his son was not able to. That afternoon the father had an amazing experience. He was sitting quietly in his usual chair in the family room when he distinctly smelled his son's favorite cigarette smoke. He whipped his head around instinctively because the scent was so apparent. It was as if he was looking for a person to physically be there smoking. There was no one there, but he knew this was his son. He had not smelled that odor in a year, and there was no explanation for how it could be there. There were no windows open, no one else was around, and any way he tried to explain it just was not possible. For the first time since his son's passing, he felt that his son was still with him, and he felt a greater comfort and hope than he could have previously imagined. This gave him the desire to learn more and try to receive more signs and messages from his son.

I tried many small rituals and practices for comfort during the first couple of years after Connor died. I kissed Connor's photo every morning and held it against my heart and did the same every evening before bed. I turned on Connor's light in his room every morning and off every evening before bed at the same time that I did so for MacKenzie and Erin. People might think that is crazy, but I missed my son more than anything I ever could have imagined and from the deepest and most desperate places of my being. This ritual seemed to comfort me just a little when I felt so helpless and in despair. My family was gracious in allowing me the space to do these activities without criticizing or questioning them.

Even with creative practices and rituals like this and all of the meetings with other bereaved parents and my grief counselor, the darkness grew darker. At about the 15-month mark, I had a counseling session with my grief therapist where I shared that I did not feel like I could go on. I was not planning on hurting myself at that point because I loved my family too much and would never abandon them. But I meant that I could not make it through more days without things changing. I explained desperately to him that I cry every single day of my life now, I cry multiple times per day, and nothing feels better without all of my children. I had done all of the "right" things, going to the various groups, journaling, therapy, and rituals of remembrance. I needed something to be fixed. I needed this awful agony to leave.

My grief counselor recommended a book called *Tracks of a Fellow Struggler*, written by Pastor John Claypool who had lost his eight-year-old daughter. My counselor spoke of the concept the pastor turned to for hope, which was the practice of gratitude. I must admit that at this point of despair, gratitude did not sound like the answer to my suffering. I was angry that the idea of gratitude could be suggested to a person with such a devastating loss. But I was desperate and had no better answer, so I read the book and thought a lot about the concept of gratitude this author presented.

One of the most difficult times to feel gratitude is when we have lost something major or precious. The conscious reminder that I had so much remaining was hopeful for me. Centering more of my mindfulness around what I had was still very difficult to do because my grief was so heavy. But it was also a new possibility that I thought might help. Following ideas I read about, I began a proactive gratitude practice. When I walked my dog each night, I practiced saying out loud as many things as I could think of to be grateful for that day. These went beyond our expected feelings of being grateful for our loved ones, our health, or our financial security. I also chose small things from each day that I could identify with gratitude. Our family had practiced a similar sharing of something we were grateful for at the dinner table every night, but we did not feel like continuing it after Connor died. That was just too hard. In order to help me remember the importance of being grateful, I kept a quote by Neale Donald Walsch on a note in my pocket and taped to my mirror. "The struggle ends when the gratitude begins." Although it was often hard to find the gratitude amidst such sorrow, this quote was a good reminder for me to keep reaching for it and trying.

At first my feelings of gratitude were tenuous when intertwined with my pain. Over time I went from being able to express gratitude for three or four things each day to 25, then 50, then 100. The thing I was grateful for could be as large as a very loving and supportive gesture from a friend or a beautiful moment with my daughters. Or it could be as small as the smell of beautiful flowers wafting towards me as I passed them on my walk. The size of the thing I was acknowledging did not matter. What was important was the expression from the heart and how it changed my energy and the way I felt. Over the next couple of years as my gratitude practice grew, I found that I could turn my energy around with this practice when I didn't know where else to turn to feel better. This active process increases a person's energetic vibration inside, and it changes how we perceive and react to the things that follow. Having an active, daily gratitude practice has become a fundamental tool for me personally and one I use in the work I do with clients.

I started adopting other new practices to help find any light during this time. While I was learning to eliminate old parts of my life that drained my energy, I was willing to try any new practices that gave me a bit of hope. As I did this, the number of signs I received from Connor increased. I continued to doubt and question the signs because it was all so new. But I did know for sure that when I received them I felt better. I felt in my heart that he was still with me. I felt connected to him, not as much as if he were still physically here with me, but connected in a new and different way. And I felt slight hope that he had not just vanished and was gone forever. At the same time, I continued to read eagerly on related topics about death. The reading I was doing now was less about individual families' tragic experiences of loss but more about their experiences of signs and their greater understanding that our loved ones are still with us. This concept was described consistently through the stories of many families and in different cultures. Although I could not have said that feeling meaningful signs from my son would help me survive this devastation, that is what began to happen.

At the time I could not talk a lot to others about these signs. I had trouble believing them myself at certain moments, and it just felt more frustrating if I had to justify them. In my heart I understood that what I was experiencing was real. But I was not ready to have someone who had never experienced them potentially discount the possibility. I could not explain how it happened, but I just knew it did. Additionally, I had experiences that were quite sacred to me, and I felt in my heart that those belonged only to Connor and me. I was still searching for the answers I needed about why God let my child die and why there was no miracle for Connor, but at least I could say I clearly felt Connor was still with me.

This time passed with an ever-changing roller coaster of deep grief and intense dark mourning. Thankfully, it was interwoven with moments of hope and light as I saw more signs from Connor and felt his presence more often. I learned that the more space I created in my life by clearing out the old things that did not serve me well anymore, the more room there was for me to slow down and notice these signs and messages. And when I would ask for more signs, amazingly, more would come. I see this happen with many others as well, whether it is a person I have worked with or other bereaved parents who have become friends. When the bereaved person makes changes and slows down, new space is created, and more and more signs can be experienced. This leads to greater hope and healing to follow.

A bereaved mom who lost her 15-year son had this experience. Her son had a severe disability and had required 24-hour daily care from the time he was born. He survived many more years than the two or three-year life expectancy the doctors initially predicted, and she dedicated her life to caring for him. While this filled her heart because she loved her son, it also was continuously draining, exhausting, and intense. After he had passed away, she worked hard to create a little more space in her life over time. She was surprised to find that when she slowed down and left open time in her days, she began to receive very clear and comforting signs from her son. This connection helped her to move forward through her pain, regret, and guilt so she could begin to feel strongly connected to her son in spirit.

I was a constantly-changing jumble of emotions. Trying to live graciously and lovingly with the family I was blessed to still have, I experienced great longing and pain that Connor was not here with us. More marking times came, and some of them were quite significant. MacKenzie was graduating from high school right before the two-year anniversary. The entire school year was filled with exciting new steps into adulthood for MacKenzie, including SAT and ACT tests, college visits, senior recognitions, and of course graduation. Erin had already completed her first two years of middle school, with so many symbolic moments of growing up, and she had become a teenager. All of these were beautiful celebratory times for our family, but they all contained a big hole as Connor was not there to share them with us. And they represented things moving forward significantly without Connor, and MacKenzie and Erin growing up rapidly without him. This dichotomy hurt me so much even amidst the many happy moments.

As I write this and a few years have passed, I have been able to find a way through the unbearable pain of our loss. This is not just because time has gone by and it heals as people often like to say. It is a result of the new foundation I created from what Connor has shown and taught me. This movement forward comes from my strong connection with Connor and deepened spiritual awareness. From this new consciousness, I have been able to take steps that have created new hope, greater healing, and deeper meaning in my life.

Family Trip to Grand Canyon, AZ;
October 2009

Connor, Erin, & MacKenzie
Family Wedding in Milwaukee, WI; June 2012

Connor Porter & Connor O'Loughlin Mantsch
Sedona, AZ; July 23, 2012

PART TWO

Healing

CHAPTER 4

Acknowledging a New Life

"We must be willing to let go of the life we planned,
so as to have the life that is waiting for us."
~ Joseph Campbell

In the earliest days of mourning, I diligently searched for research, inspirational writings, people's personal stories of loss, historical perspectives on tragic death, poetry, or any source of information that could provide greater meaning. I needed anything that could lead me to some understanding of what had happened. The last thing I wanted was a new life when I was thoroughly happy with the one that I had been blessed with and built. But there it was, and that's what I had.

What this traumatic loss did to me is hard to explain. Linda, who was the Director of the Grief Counseling Program at French's Funeral Home, met with us in the days right after the accident. She spoke to us gently and softly at the time explaining to us what was going on in a way that both Bryan and I might comprehend in our shock. She said that our brains are like a file cabinet where each experience gives us a "folder" or context in which to place the new experiences of our lives so that we can understand them. When something happens as traumatic as your son being killed in an airplane crash and never returning home, there just is no folder or even a file cabinet for that. There was no context to comprehend what to do with an experience that was so painful, abnormal, and completely unexpected. This description helped explain why we could not absorb basic sentences, words, or ideas at that time. It helped us to better understand the fogginess and lack of cognition we were both having, which made us feel very paralyzed and helpless.

Linda recommended that we explore grief counseling and family support. She gave us a packet with lists of resources such as support organizations, books, and online sites that could assist us. Like everything else at the time, it made no sense to me. It was like I was trying to read Latin because I could not comprehend anything and had no context for it. I just wanted to know how I could get Connor back and end the terrible agony I felt.

I glanced at the sheet of paper. There were many words I recognized like "frequent tears," "lack of energy," and "anger" that all made sense to me. The word "God" was mentioned and "finding support" and "taking care of oneself." These phrases were all fairly intuitive even if meaningless to me at the time. There was one word I remember that stood out. The word was "reconciliation." It felt stupid and obscure to me at the moment. It felt so out of place compared to the other soft and loving words on the sheet.

This word irritated me enough that I kept looking at it, and I asked Linda more about it. I was not ready to learn at that time how the word God might still apply to my life or whether prayer had any role in my life when Connor was gone. So this strange word that seemed harsh and out of context confused me.

When I asked Linda about it, she said that I should not worry too much about that right now. It was a concept for later. She said that my path through this new world of grief would be varied and different depending on the point in time from my loss and the support that I received. This answer kind of bothered me, so I pressed her for more about that word. She described to me that reconciliation was the process of learning to live with a loss and integrating that loss into your life. It was a theoretical explanation as she danced softly around the pain it might cause me. But I quickly got it. I said, "So you are suggesting that in time I will accept this?" I was crushed and angry and could barely speak. She answered, "It is not an acceptance necessarily but rather an integration." There was nowhere for me to file this information. It was impossible. All I could hear was that the Universe somehow expected me to arrive at a point someday where I would say I accept this and it is okay. This was repulsive to me.

I have never forgotten the shock and pain of that word at the time. But what was probably harder was when I realized into the second year that this word reconciliation was real. I did not necessarily like the word any more than I did when I initially heard it. And I avoided any thought of it throughout the first year and a half because it was too painful of a thing to ask of me. But I came to a point where I realized this process was necessary even if I still hated the fact that it would be required of me. I was considering that acknowledging this new life and finding a way to integrate the loss of my precious son might be necessary if I were to ever come out of the black hole that I felt entrapped me daily. I did not know how, but intuitively it seemed like I had little choice and that something better might come again in the future if I could.

One mother I worked with had lost her young daughter and experienced the challenges of not acknowledging her new life after the early years had passed. While it is typical to receive physical items from people in the early years that are in honor of our loved one who died, generally this subsides after the first few years. We received loving scrapbooks, photo albums, team jerseys in honor and memory of Connor, and other physical recognitions of his life and passing. These were beautiful comforts in the early years, and we were so grateful for each and every one of them. It was normal, however, that we received fewer over time. This particular woman desperately wanted to continue collecting many physical items in honor of her daughter, and her daughter's room was overflowing with the new things that had been added in addition to the items her daughter had in her room. Acquiring more and more items created pain for the rest of her family because it hindered their ability to learn to live without the daughter. They wanted to reduce the items by sharing the girl's things with people who needed them while keeping the most special items to cherish. With help, this mother learned that collecting so many new items for her daughter kept her from acknowledging her new life, and this was complicating her grieving and her connection with those she loved. She learned to seek more internal recognitions of her daughter's life through writing poetry, putting together commemorative albums, and creating a memorial scholarship fund while condensing the physical items they kept. This transition helped her whole family move forward together while incorporating the daughter they lost into their new life.

Many additional losses can result when we don't move forward through the difficult process of acknowledging our new life. I was familiar with the detrimental effects that profound grief can have on a person and was worried about that for myself. Experiencing this torture inside every day, I could see that my health was being greatly affected. All of the horrific pain I felt in my heart and soul was manifesting in my body. I had terrible pains in my back, neck, and shoulders. By the middle of each day, I felt like I had lifted boulders all day long when I had not lifted a thing. I had pains radiating up the tops of my arms from my hands. My sleep was never restful and my eyes were bloodshot each day, which reflected the turmoil and anguish inside of me while I slept. I had headaches daily. I would hate to try and recall how many Advil I took the first year to stave off these pains. And my energy level felt like I was 25 years older than I was.

MacKenzie and Erin were the strongest reasons to push myself toward acknowledgment of this new life when it was the last thing I wanted to do. Children learn far more from what we do than what we say. Regardless of their age, they repeat what we do without even knowing it themselves. I was beginning to see what MacKenzie and Erin were learning from me on this grief journey. Many things were good, and I worked hard to set the example that it was healthy for us to speak openly and authentically about Connor and that we would never forget him. We tried to laugh and share the many funny stories about him. I shared my pain when it was appropriate, so they could see that it is normal and healthy. And they learned that expressing pain is critical to the healing process. I reached hard for gratitude and graciousness at times when I was feeling anger and envy for people who still had their sons when I did not.

But I saw areas that needed improvement. MacKenzie and Erin wanted to do things that were normal for kids to do. They wanted to take photographs of our family and the two of them while the thought of having any photo missing one of my children pained me. They wanted to do family activities that we used to do and found enjoyable, and they wanted to laugh again. They wanted to experience the moments of their growing up that were rightfully theirs. Eventually, MacKenzie and Erin had wanted me to stop setting a place at the kitchen table in remembrance of Connor, a practice that comforted me through the early months. I wasn't ready, but I did it for them. I could see that while it was soothing to me, it felt awkward to them, and it was blocking a step of acknowledgment of our changed family.

One of the hardest things for me to learn to say were the words "Connor died" or "my son died," or "Connor was dead." I could say "I lost my son," and I could say "Connor was killed." But something about the word died was too painful, too ugly, too raw and stabbing. While this avoidance was understandable early on, as time passed MacKenzie and Erin became uncomfortable with the lengths I would go to avoid those words. Without realizing it, I was teaching them an avoidance pattern that was not healthy and could be harmful to them later.

One of the things I wanted to avoid at all costs was becoming a shell of a person. I had known a person like this and had already met others like this at a conference I attended. One woman who had lost her 23-year-old daughter to cancer struggled very much with acknowledging her changed life. Her body continued to function as she took care of basic motherly duties like driving the other children to their appointments, watching sporting events, and periodically cleaning up the house. But she remained bitter and angry for years and years later. Her body moved around in the world, but there was only an angry and closed heart inside. This was a painful experience for everyone who knew her. So much more of her life was lost year after year, and she suffered even further as did those closest to her. I knew I never wanted to become like this. Despite how much I did not want to acknowledge this new life without Connor, speaking with her and seeing her suffering decades later increased my determination to find a way.

I faced many obstacles while trying to get more comfortable with acknowledging what I didn't choose, never wanted, and vehemently hated. The first one was fear. One of the greatest fears for a bereaved parent is that people are going to forget their child. I have heard this from every bereaved parent I have met. This fear is partly why we create foundations or memorial funds in our children's names. This fear is often why we create 5K runs, research drives, or other memorial events in our children's names. MacKenzie hand designed mugs for us as Christmas gifts the first year that said, "Connor's Mom" or "Connor's Aunt." These were beautiful and treasured by each of us. Connor's cousin, Tiffany, made t-shirts in honor of Connor's musical ability and love of Shakespeare. They were his favorite color red, had his name on one side, and had a quote by Shakespeare written on the other side, "If music be the food of love, play on." MacKenzie and Erin made t-shirts in Connor's honor that said "What Would Connor Do?" to demonstrate his unusually strong integrity and character and remind us to make decisions in our lives that would honor Connor. Every single effort someone took to remember Connor soothed my heart just a little, which is why acknowledging our new life without him was so difficult. If I acknowledged this more fully, I feared Connor and the important gifts he brought to the world might be forgotten.

Another issue I struggled with was that acknowledging Connor's death seemed to encourage people to act like he never existed. I noticed just two or three years after Connor died, people said Connor's name less and less, told fewer stories about him, and sent fewer notes letting me know they had been thinking about him or us. What would happen five years out or ten or twenty? Would my precious son not exist to people anymore? How would I aid that the more I started to truly acknowledge and take steps toward living a different and new life that did not include Connor? This really worried me. And I thought as Connor's mom I was primarily responsible for helping the world to know him and remember what he meant here, since he and his life were too special to be forgotten.

Fearing that your child will be forgotten if you move forward is very painful, and you may feel you will lose your child even more. It is very possible for you to keep your child in your life even with greater acknowledgment of your new physical life without him. In addition to keeping your child's memories alive in a physical way, you can also create a new and different relationship with your child in spirit. There are different ways to do this, and information is provided at the end of the book to help you learn how.

One of the areas that was the most arduous and took the longest for me as a mother to "reconcile" was how my identity instantly changed when I lost one of my children. When Connor died, I had already been a mother for 16 years, and specifically, I was a mother of three children. I was the mother of two girls and a boy. I had both boys and girls, and we had a family of five. These things were my identity and I loved them. They defined one of the most beautiful parts of who I was. I loved being a family of five, a mother of three, a mother who had both genders, and a mother of a son. It was perfect for me. Who and what did I become on July 26, 2012? This question angered and confused me. All of a sudden, I wasn't those things anymore even though this is all I had known. How could I actively acknowledge this new life and existence when everything I knew about myself and loved for so long had instantly changed?

I was also experiencing the bizarre phenomenon of meeting new people who did not know me before the accident. When they didn't hear me talk about a boy, they assumed I had two children and a single gender, daughters. I was suddenly out of a club that I had belonged to for over 14 years, that of mothers of sons, and all of the funny stories and things it entailed. When people talked about the huge feet or stinky tennis shoes of their teenaged sons, I still felt part of that club. But they could not see it because Connor was no longer here. When I was automatically excluded from that club, I felt like I did not know on what planet I existed. And I wanted to scream to them, "I know about stinky tennis shoes, and Connor had a size 11 1/2 shoe by age 14." And when mothers joked about how much food they went through in their house and how many gallons of milk their boys drank, I wanted to tell them how it was the same for me. But all of a sudden it was not anymore. I wanted to tell them how when Connor was here we went through five gallons of milk each week and the checkout guy at Walgreens knew us because we were the only ones who stopped in and bought four gallons at a time. It mattered so much to me because this was the person I had always been and the life I knew. And I loved these funny realities about our life. But people didn't seem to want to talk about a life that was or about a person who once was here but is no longer. And that was another crushing blow. Years of my life felt like they were being erased in an instant as if they never had existed. Every step of acknowledgment that I made felt like I was falling deeper and darker into confusion and away from the life I knew, chose, and wanted to cling to. I wasn't sure I wanted any part of the whole acknowledgment and reconciliation thing regardless of any apparent benefit.

Acknowledgment for anyone who is bereaved, and particularly for a parent who has lost a child, is a choice and a step that is much bigger than it may seem. Acknowledging meant opening up space to see this new life I had been given without my son and really feeling it. Feeling what it felt like from every angle and trying it on through every experience and circumstance of each day, no matter how much it hurt. And it hurt constantly. Every time I wanted to avoid it, I tried to look at the reasons why I had to do it. MacKenzie and Erin were two of my biggest reasons. The honest truth is that if I had not had them, the shell option was pretty damn appealing. But watching them grow up each day as life continued on helped me to see some light through this nonstop struggle.

My greatest blessings through this stage were the increasing number of signs I received from Connor that let me know he was still with me, and he supported and encouraged this acknowledgment. I could tell with each sign or message and in the way that it came, that acknowledging my new life without him here did not leave him behind. Although Connor was not physically present, he was still integrated into our lives and very much remained a part of our days.

Often a grieving parent hears the suggestion that her pain will be helped and her family will be best served when she can "move on." This statement almost never comes from someone who has lost a child. While well-intended, it is usually said because the person does not know what else to say or is having a hard time continuing to hear and talk about the loss. They are the ones who want to move on because it is too painful to keep hearing about it and they don't want to feel helpless. It is really a reflection that the person is blessed to not understand why this is so painful to do. Suggestions that the bereaved person is not moving on quickly enough usually only serve to intensify the person's pain, suffering, isolation, and guilt.

"Moving on" usually means to move on without your child. He is not physically here so the remaining physical family unit must move on without him. It is left brain thinking - logical, practical, and considers only what our eyes can see and our intellect can explain and prove. What I have been blessed to learn is that this is not the way it has to be. This concept of leaving our loved one behind is not the only way we can live our changed life. The term I finally settled on that I could stomach, say, and believe with my heart was to "move forward." This distinction may sound small, but it is actually very large. Moving forward leaves a lot of room to take Connor with me and for our family to do so. This means his existence did not end, and his time here was not necessarily cut short. I am still a mother of a son, a mother of three, and Connor still has a role in our lives. We do not delude ourselves into thinking he is still here physically. I no longer set a place for Connor each night at the dinner table, I don't ask for a table for five at a restaurant any longer, and I don't say that I need an extra rollaway bed when I book a hotel room because I have three children. These things still sear and ache every time

I must face them. But Connor does truly move forward with us each day in a different way. He gives signs and messages that show us he is with us at the brightest and most beautiful moments we experience as well as during the times that we drop back into the abyss, often unprepared and unsuspecting of the trigger. I talk to him both in my times of need for help and when I just want to laugh at a memory or feel close to him. In the moments when I still experience and feel Connor, I find beauty. When I am asked by the Universe to take this painful step of acknowledgment, I also have a new way to keep Connor with me.

When Connor was alive, I was his cheerleader. I loved being physically present at all of his games and practices. I was also a cheerleader through all of the moments of his personal life and through the normal pains and trials he had as an adolescent boy who was becoming a young man. And now Connor is my cheerleader. I would never have imagined it, but he comforts me just when I need him most because I have learned to experience and feel him. He picks me up by providing a sign when I cannot go on another moment. He keeps guiding me forward showing me there is something more I am working toward even if I cannot yet see it clearly.

Following a dramatic life change, especially one of significant loss, you need new ways of seeing and making sense of your life. There are deeper ways to understand loss, tragedy, and change that come from shifting perspectives from what you may have always learned or thought. If you would like suggestions on where to start, information is provided at the back of the book to help you.

CHAPTER 5

Acknowledging a New You

"The greatest glory in living is not in never falling, but in rising every time we fall."

~ Nelson Mandela

Through the early stages of mourning, I had a slight reprieve to the agonizing pain when other people were quietly with me. But as soon as people left, the pain would rush in, and I would be back in the abyss. As my grief journey changed with the seasons, people resumed their own lives. My pain became more private, and I had to go deeper within myself to deal with the feelings of desolation and despair. I did not know how to do this and felt very alone.

This new life was confusing and daunting. Although I looked similar on the outside, I felt like most of who I was had changed into someone I didn't know or understand. It seemed like I had a few original foundation pieces of myself left that joined with all sorts of new parts and pieces I did not recognize. I could see that my former ways of going about daily living no longer fit because the very ways in which I saw and understood life were so different. This realization required that I create new practices and ways of living even though this felt like I was leaving more of my old self and old life behind. This felt scary, but it seemed time to give myself permission to do things that I did not necessarily do before and be things that I would not have necessarily chosen before. I needed to figure out what fit this new me who I was just getting to know.

Before I lost a child, I had plenty of energy to focus on a vigorous exercise routine, to perform at a very high level every day at work, and to enjoy many outside activities for entertainment. I liked to go to a movie or a live performance, eat a lovely dinner out, or cook a wonderful meal at home with family and friends. With the much lower energy level I had now, I didn't care much about most of those things, and the mere thought of the energy required to go out to a nice restaurant or a show was exhausting. I was very vulnerable, and my pain was still so raw. My energy was consumed by working, taking care of my family, helping us all through our grief, and trying to care for my shattered heart a little each day. I didn't want to feel like I was losing more of myself, but I recognized that I had to reduce the expectations I had for myself and my perceptions of who I needed to be.

I had previously trained for and competed in triathlons, maintaining a challenging weekly exercise regimen. I enjoyed the challenge and it fed my spirit. It also balanced out my intensity from being more of a Type A person. By the time of the accident, a solid exercise routine had been an engrained part of my life for over 20 years. It was part of who I was, but I was feeling unnecessary pressure and a lack of enjoyment continuing in this way. Still, it was hard to imagine changing one more thing that was familiar.

After Connor died, people told me I should walk. I didn't get it. I could hardly get out of bed in the morning and had no desire to wander anywhere. Walking sounded not only unappealing but also kind of like a waste of precious time. If I was to do anything, I should go for a long run or get in a good workout to stay a step ahead of looming full depression, which felt like it might consume me at any time. I tried it anyway because I was willing to try most anything people would suggest that could possibility help. It did not take very long for me to discover that there was value in it. The forward movement, but without the heart and foot pounding intensity during a run, metaphorically moved me just a tiny bit forward. I began to walk my dog, Asia, more days per week and exercise intensely fewer days. Worries about my fitness level fell a little more to the background, and I was surprised to find that I received more frequent and larger signs during these walks. I suspected this happened because I was not in as much of a hurry like I was when running, and I was able to notice them more.

One of the early signs I saw on a walk strikes me more strongly today than when I was still quite numb to everything around me at that time. My favorite place to walk Asia was through the open space of our high school, which was only a five-minute walk from our house. It was quiet, and I would rarely encounter many other people while walking the paths. Depending on the time of day, I could see the sunrise, sunset, a sky full of stars, or the beautiful Sandia Mountain range. I typically walked the paths in the exact same way each time because this was one less decision I needed to make amidst a life of too many new and overwhelming decisions.

On one part of the trail, three beautiful full and very tall trees stood in a row that lined a side of the school's tennis courts. Albuquerque is a high desert climate, so huge, leafy trees are not prevalent in the middle of the city. I always took special notice and appreciated them when I passed by. One day my eye was particularly drawn to them, and I noticed the strangest thing. The leaves on the tree in the middle were moving, waving, and shimmering beautifully. Then I realized that it was only the leaves on the middle tree that moved, and the leaves of the two trees immediately on each side of it were completely still. I looked around me because I had not thought it was very windy that day, and it was then that I realized there was no breeze at all. And there were no other trees in the vicinity with leaves that were moving. It was a very still day. Despite the fact that I did not know what to make of this at that time, my heart instinctively felt something beautiful. Right before I looked up, I had been crying and was very despairing and sad. I had been missing Connor intensely and painfully. Connor was always deeply connected to nature, trees, and all things that grew. It felt healing and comforting when I noticed the tree. For that brief moment I felt Connor deeply, and I felt a beauty that I could not explain but knew was an act of grace beyond physical understanding.

I had gained some weight after the first year once I began to fully recognize the pain and burden of a life without Connor. I really didn't care all that much at the time. This apathy was unusual for me, and I wanted to care, but I didn't. There was not an ounce of my being that had the energy to deprive myself of anything through a diet or obsess over what I ate when my soul felt the darkness of the greatest deprivation a mother could experience. I am glad that this later reversed, and I came back to my normal weight that made me feel more like myself. But early on I needed to avoid anything that made me feel anymore deprived than I already felt.

I came to a point in the second year where I was ready to break. It was a very heavy load to hold the Chief Operating Officer position I had at my company, continue to raise my family, and learn how to live this new life as a bereaved mom who desperately missed her son each and every day. Most days I failed to meet the normal standards I set for myself for work performance, and it was one more thing that felt overwhelming and made me disappointed in myself. I wanted to be more than I could find my way to be at that time, but I also knew that there were bigger things I needed to focus on given the enormity of what had happened.

I gave the best I had at work and cared very much about my company and co-workers. I had been the first person hired at the company and had been responsible for helping it develop and expand. After much thought, I requested to work a shorter workweek that was 75 percent of my full-time schedule. Permitting myself to do this was difficult because I had an important role that I had been proud of. I did not take that lightly, and I had never been a quitter. Whatever was tossed my way, I found a way to get through it. It felt like I was letting people down and not trying hard enough to keep up with everything I had previously done. But I had to be realistic about the amount of energy I now possessed, and my energy needed to be spread much further and in new directions. While I was hesitant to take this step, it helped create an opening I needed to begin new rituals for myself, and it was a step toward healing and healthier choices later on.

I also stepped back from a few of the responsibilities that I had outside of work and family. I had always been an active member of the Parent Association Board at our middle and high school, chairing a different committee each year or serving a different role on the Executive Committee. I was similarly active at our kids' grade schools and on community boards. The accident happened three weeks before school was to begin in the fall, and I took a position the previous spring as Chairperson of a large, year-long committee. Although I wanted to fulfill that commitment, it was too much even to think about continuing with. I gave myself permission to step down from that role and asked them to replace me. This was not an easy decision because it served Erin's grade, and she was starting new at the school. But I needed to lift a little of the weight from my shoulders with all I had to deal with.

There is an incredible freedom that comes from allowing yourself to be right where you are whether or not anyone can understand it from the outside. This is a personal journey, and each grieving person's path is different. You have the right to define that for yourself. When you can begin to let go of the things that no longer serve you, space will be created to begin new rituals and practices that you now need more.

Once I gave myself permission to let go of some of the old, I had space to let in new things. A few of my rituals and practices were small and others were larger. One thing we did early on was to include Connor in our prayer before we ate. When the children were young, we created a dinner prayer that expressed our gratitude for the blessings we had and for the natural world and greater Universe in which we exist. We added a sentence to the end that expressed our love for Connor and our gratitude that we had him in our lives here as long as we did. This inclusion was a helpful way for me to let go of my need to set a place for Connor at the dinner table yet kept him with us in a way each evening.

I made it a point to go to church more frequently. I had attended fairly regularly before the accident, but I craved spiritual connection much more after Connor died. It was a double-edged sword. I cried every time I went to church even in the second year and into the third. Being in a sacred place and feeling with my spirit and heart released all that had been bottled up during the work week. At first, I was very uncomfortable and tried to stuff down the tears or just not attend at all even if I needed it. But then I gave myself permission to not care. If anyone who didn't know me asked why I wept each week in church, they would surely understand with little explanation. And those who knew me clearly knew why. I desperately needed anything that could open my heart, move my spirit, and make me feel like I was still alive inside, and being at a church service helped do this.

The gratitude practice that I had started earlier following discussions with my grief counselor became more rooted. I continued doing this primarily each night when I walked, but I did it at other times, too. I noticed that I received more signs when I did my gratitude practice while walking than I did if I just walked or talked on the phone while I walked. My energy and vibration always rose when I committed that time to expressing my gratitude. This opened me up, and I began to more easily notice signs.

Another new ritual I added was reading every night before going to sleep. Making time for reading was challenging because the heavy load I carried with work and family meant that I went to bed usually after 11:30 each night and was quite exhausted as I laid down to read. But reading and learning more was really important to me. If I only lasted for 15 minutes, I still never wanted to miss it. MacKenzie and Erin would tease me because they often found my light on, but I was sound asleep with my book on my lap. I tended to read books that explained what I was going through, that shared experiences of bereaved people finding happiness again, or stories of people who had near-death experiences or miracles occur in their lives. All of these topics gave me a better understanding of what I was going through and more hope for my future.

This reading time was another way that Connor could send me signs and messages. He did it in two ways. First, there was a spot on the roof that would sound like there was a knocking on it periodically. This was odd because it seemed pretty impossible that anything could be making noise since there was nothing up there. It was always in the same spot, and it was central enough that we could hear it from most rooms in the house. It happened over and over again when it had never previously happened in that house, and I began to suspect there may not be a physical explanation for it. I did not know what to make of this possibility, so I went up on the roof one day to check it out. I saw that there was nothing that could be making that noise. There weren't any tree branches that could reach to the center, there were no birds or animal nests, nor were there any units like air conditioners or ducts in the ceiling there. It was totally an open space. Bryan heard it frequently as well and also felt that the noises from that spot were signs from Connor.

I began to notice a pattern to the noises that more clearly let me know it was Connor. I learned to look down and notice exactly what I was reading at the moment the sound occurred. The sound typically occurred when I was reading about a person's experiences with signs from a loved one who had passed. Or the sound would happen when I was reading about the extensive research on people with near-death experiences or people who have experienced true miracles. In those accounts the person would describe what the afterlife, Heaven, or God was like. I learned that these accounts tended to be very similar, and Connor was giving me messages about which parts I should pay attention to. These messages always answered questions I desperately wondered about like how he was, if he was okay and happy, what was it like where he was, and if I could ever hope to be with him again.

The second way Connor sent me signs or messages while I read was by messing with my light or smoke detector battery. I began to notice that there were times when my light would flicker on and off, and there was no correlation to anything happening like a storm or wind outside, a burned out light bulb, or too much energy usage in our house. Similarly, there were times when the smoke detector battery would tweet that had no correlation to a battery beginning to wear out. I always explored the logical and practical explanations for these things because I only wanted to place hope where I could be certain I would not be disappointed later. And with the knocking, the lights, and the smoke detector battery, there clearly were not physical explanations for them. As I got better at recognizing the signs more quickly, my ability to interpret and understand them improved. I was receiving important messages Connor wanted me to know, which gave me much greater peace, hope, and possibility.

During this time, I needed to find ways to help soothe my heart and senses since grief makes them feel so heavily overloaded. This was particularly important during times when I dropped back into the feelings of darkness and hopelessness and had difficulty bringing myself back out. Over time, I developed a self-care "tool kit." I kept a list of anything that gave me momentary pleasure that could help in those frequent, painful moments of helplessness. My tool kit was personal as these were just things that I enjoyed and that helped to calm my senses in that moment. It contained the following:

- Texting for a short time with someone I loved
- Enjoying an exceptional cup of coffee that I stopped to appreciate
- Having a call with a friend or one of my sisters
- Taking a comforting and soothing bath
- Watching a gentle or hopeful movie
- Sipping a glass of good wine
- Listening to songs about loss that connected me with others who shared this experience
- Reading articles or books about grief and what comes after we die
- Enjoying a piece of delicious dark chocolate
- Listening to Connor's piano compositions that he created
- Listening to classical or Native American flute music to soothe my heart

Some of these things gave me momentary soothing or comfort and others helped drown out the painful noise inside my head. Certain ones helped me to feel something, anything that moved my heart and spirit.

Turning to these comforts gave me a small measure of control that I desperately needed when nothing could give me what I really wanted, which was to have both Connor and my old life back again. These small things did help. There were days I needed one or two. Other days I needed them all and a few of them more than once. There were days none of them helped, but it was powerful in that it was a support I created and allowed myself to enjoy when I needed it. Nobody could take these things away from me, and they were not harmful to anyone.

These steps of permissions and rituals were really important markers on my journey to greater healing and spiritual expansion. Tragedy helps us to know better what truly matters and can guide us to redefine our priorities. I could see how these small decisions were doing that. I knew if I did not try to balance my pain with small moments of comfort that the possibility of rebelling in a greater way was more likely. It is not uncommon for people who are deeply bereaved to quit their job in a moment of anger, sell their house, move cities, have an affair, or do any other extreme measure to bring back the control that feels unfairly taken away.

Although these steps were small, they were important building blocks toward moving into this new life with a little choice. They were openings to the greater beauty that would later unfold. These new openings invited more connection with Connor and gave room for me to experience more signs and messages. These steps then led to a stronger spiritual connection with God than I ever imagined was possible.

Acknowledging that you are different and not the same person as you were before your loss is important. Taking steps to define the new person you are becoming can help you become more comfortable with this change that was not your choice. We can choose to make changes in how we physically keep ourselves, how we share immediate family responsibilities, how we relate to our extended family with their accompanying expectations and traditions, how we choose to live our professional and work lives, as well as in other ways. If you would like help exploring which areas you wish to keep and which you may want to redefine, information is provided at the back of the book that can help you begin.

CHAPTER 6

Creating Space for Something New

"A wound is the place where light enters you."
~ Rumi

W ith the new steps I was taking, I realized that I needed more open space in my life. I needed more quiet time, more time for reading, more opportunity to learn about the experiences of others on this path, and more thinking and reflective time. I needed more space to figure out how to keep Connor moving forward with us, and I felt more of a need to do something to help others given all that I had tumultuously experienced. It seemed that something new and good would have to come eventually or I would not survive. And all of Connor's signs and messages reinforced this to me even during the moments when it was difficult to believe or hope that anything good could possibly come again.

There were a number of ways in which I created space in my life for something new. Meditation and yoga were two of the main things I tried. I had always wanted to learn to meditate and to practice yoga more frequently. These were on my "should" list as I was raising my children because I heard about all of the benefits of doing these. Before Connor died, I felt too busy running here and there and raising my family to incorporate those slower practices into my life. But old ways of living were no longer working well and most often did not feel right. I decided it was finally time to learn more about both of these practices. Neither was very easy for me at first because I was not very patient, my mind was still foggy, and my grief still made concentrating quite difficult. It took a long time before I received greater benefits from these practices and understood more why I was doing them. I kept trying them, however, and over time I got better and better.

The yoga and meditation required me to slow down, and I began to better examine the ways in which I chose to spend my time. I no longer had any tolerance for activities that felt like a waste of time or for people who drained my energy, and I made new choices that honored these feelings. While I wasn't rude, I just could not stomach these things. One example was sitting through meetings that were unproductive and negative. Another was participating in groups or on committees only because I felt I should when they didn't connect to my heart or relate to the new things I was going through. People who talked on and on about situations they could easily change but chose not to angered me when I could never change this deeply despairing and cavernous loss. I still empathized with others, but I kept those interactions short and passed whenever I could on more superficial things. I also stopped watching the news for a while. Although I risked sounding a little less knowledgeable about current events, there was little that was very significant that I could not catch up with if needed. My heart couldn't tolerate the hurt and abuse that goes on in our world and is reported day after day. I was still too raw and vulnerable, and I had no room to feel more pain that I could not do anything about.

People periodically pushed back when I tried to make these changes. I think this was not intentional but happened for a couple of reasons. My looking deeper and choosing in ways that were different prompted others to ask similar questions about their own lives that could feel uncomfortable. Also, many people wanted the same Shari they knew before. They wanted to have the old me back that they knew and felt a loss when I was making a change that seemed to them to take more of the old Shari away.

When your child dies, much of who you are dies, too. When Connor died, I felt like I had lost a chunk of my heart, my soul, and at least one limb. This is how it truly felt. Profound loss is felt physically, mentally, emotionally, spiritually, and metaphysically. Because of Connor's signs and my spiritual deepening that resulted, I can say that I like a lot of parts of the new Shari that has emerged. And I think others do too. But there was a period of time when I wasn't sure who might emerge to replace the old me who no longer existed, and this was a scary feeling.

Space started opening up in my life as I tried a variety of new and different things. One of the things I turned to first was writing. I started with writing poetry and prose about the pain of my loss and the changes I was experiencing. Then my writing expanded to helpful information around loss and bereavement. Knowing we had been through this experience, people began to ask me how they could support others close to them who were grieving. This led me to create a list of helpful suggestions to share with others. People wanted to know how I was experiencing signs from Connor, so I created a list of the ways others could begin to identify signs. The writing created space because I would have a rush of new ideas, perspectives, and understandings that I didn't realize were inside of me whenever I began writing. It slowed me down, and a lot of new things came from it. Over time, I realized how much meaning I derived from helping others, and these small actions became larger ones that led me to modify my work a few years later to help support others in their healing.

Another way I created space was through driving. I was blessed to have Erin and MacKenzie with me who were still active, growing teenagers. MacKenzie had just left for college in Denver, Colorado, and Erin was at home. MacKenzie and I remained very close, so she welcomed opportunities for me to come to Denver, see her new life, and participate in activities organized by the university and parent's association. Denver is a seven-hour drive from Albuquerque, and I chose whenever possible to drive instead of fly. The time driving by myself in the beautiful expansiveness of New Mexico and Colorado filled me up and helped me to breathe more deeply. Since I was idle behind the wheel for hours each way, I was able to open up creative space and increase my mindfulness when otherwise my day would have been filled with busy activities and daily tasks.

As Erin was getting older, she was participating in team sports at school. I had the enjoyment of watching her games for different sports during the various seasons. Many of these games were at other schools located one or two hours away, and she also had weekend tournaments in Denver or other cities located five to seven hours away. I had the same experience of being filled up and expanded when I sat idle during drives to these sports activities, too. Many new perspectives, ideas, and possibilities began to emerge.

I wanted to deepen my spiritual understanding and knowledge during this time. This led me to increasing the time I devoted to reading. I gravitated to all sorts of things including nonfiction books and spiritual texts, works of the philosophers I had studied long ago, as well as websites, blogs, and publications of experts or individuals who had unique experiences. I was interested in things that supported what I felt spiritually as well as ideas that challenged what I thought I knew. Suddenly, so much opened up as I saw the variety of information and knowledge I could access about the very painful questions I had. As I read and learned more, I realized that I was finding companionship in areas that really mattered and were meaningful to me. For the first time, pieces of me that had shut down tightly after the trauma of losing Connor were curious and began to open up a little bit more. There were even moments of enthusiasm when I read information that hit home or explained something I was really struggling with. Many new paths stemmed from this as I later transitioned my work in a way that connected my personal interests and activities with my professional ones and helped me start to feel life again.

Walking more and increasing the amount of time I spent in nature was an additional way I created space for something new. Research has shown the great benefits we receive from spending time in nature. We open up, expand, and relax when in nature in ways that are difficult to do when we are in our daily and weekly routine. Connor and our family always cherished time in nature, and we chose to spend time this way as a part of our traditions. We were fortunate to live less than a mile from the base of the Sandia Mountains and had many choices of hiking trails easily accessible. We shared a favorite hiking trail that was a 15-minute drive from our house, which all of us really enjoyed including our dog, Asia. Because nature was such a huge part of Connor's life, it was one of the places we could feel his presence most strongly. Whenever I walked or hiked I received signs from Connor, and this affirmation was critical to my path forward. Breathing in the fresh air, relishing the sunshine on my face, seeing the beauty of the mountains encompassing me, and feeling my son's presence provided a momentary reprieve and slight relief from the heartache. Hiking created space for many new things as my perspective and mood shifted allowing more possibilities to surface in my awareness. Many times when I received a sign from Connor, it felt like an affirmation of what I had been thinking about or considering, and new things started opening up. I processed bigger decisions when I walked or hiked and frequently practiced gratitude.

Gardening was another way I created space for something new. I started vegetable gardening with Connor when he was around the age of six. In those early years, I did most of the work while he curiously explored how things were connected to the earth, what made them grow, and how life was sustained. He happily chatted away next to me while I worked expressing his wondrous discoveries to me and to himself. He liked to tell me why certain vegetables grew quickly and easily and why we could not manage to get other ones to grow after repeated attempts.

As the children got older and I got busier, Connor took on more of the work. He loved to do this. Being in nature and using his hands in the natural world gave him peace and much-needed thinking time. He was really good at it, and we were blessed with large gardens that produced delicious tomatoes, beans, cucumbers, herbs, melons, corn, and more. In the spring of 2012 before his trip to Sedona, Connor had planted an extra-large garden that flourished. We were blessed that autumn with the abundant food he had grown with his own hands after he was no longer here to share it with us.

After the accident it was painful for me to even think about gardening without Connor much less attempt it. I was so sad when the last of the vegetables from that season were gone, and I knew I would never again have vegetables grown from the love and energy of his heart and hands. As with so many things that Connor and I shared over the years, going forward it would just be me. After many painful attempts, I began to slowly try another garden. The first one I planted was small and a lot less impressive than were Connor's. I couldn't figure out how he had hooked up all of the automatic sprinklers nor could I easily haul the heavy bags of soil to the back of the house like he did. Many things were harder. Although painful to do alone, I realized that gardening also brought me greater peace. I felt a strong connection to Connor while I worked even if this was sometimes through tears.

Gardening became a very helpful activity to create space for something new. At times I had to crawl between and behind large plants to pick the vegetables or tend to things. I would discover new things by going behind, through, and under what I couldn't see in front of me. While weaving in and out of small spaces to pick the vegetables, I realized this process was a metaphor for my life now without Connor. The way I discovered most things on this painful journey was by going behind, around, under, and through the pain, even when I could not see what was in front of me, to find what might be on the other side. I had to weave in and out of hard to see areas, at times succeeding and at other times not. And I had to get my hands really dirty by digging deeply into the earth in order to produce any results. The same was true for my grief journey. Over time I was able to strongly feel Connor's presence and experience signs from him when I was deeply rooted and connected to the earth in this way. It seemed to be his way of continuing with me in this activity that we adored and shared.

Finally, I spent more small moments just being and not always doing something. This is not necessarily typical in today's world when many of us are overly stretched and life is full of so many activities. Nor is it regularly rewarded to just be and not do. I would sit in the car for a short time before I went into the next place I was off to, or I paused a few moments longer once I returned home from a series of activities. Other times I sat outside in my garden or on a bench with a view for a few minutes longer than I normally would. I regularly had music on in the background when I did things, but now I would take more time to stop and listen to the music and really hear the words or melody that was playing. I still was very busy with work and family so none of these were long periods of time. But I was amazed at how five to fifteen minutes of space to sit quietly made a big difference in my day. These moments helped calm my agitated heart and nerves, which were still so acutely raw from the trauma. Increasing those small moments of silence and stillness created space for many new things.

Have you incorporated new habits, practices, or rituals into your life that have provided peace or momentary comfort? Have you wanted to make changes or develop new practices but are not sure where to start? If you would like to explore new activities or practices that may bring you comfort and better fit you and your life now, resources are provided at the end of the book that will help you.

Creating space for something new is critical because we need to make room for what will emerge newly within us. Through silence and stillness, we can better hear the insights and truths of our soul. An important opening for healing begins here because we can then connect to our inner wisdom and divine guidance, which shows us the way.

CHAPTER 7

Feeling Your Loved One is Still With You

"Through the sounds of a breeze, through a whisper from a star, through the spirit of the trees, through a ray of sun, I feel you."

~ Unknown

The more we can feel our loved one in spirit, the more we can trust that there is something beyond us. After experiencing Connor's presence more frequently, I started to have greater faith that there still was a God even if I could not answer painful questions such as why God would let my innocent child suffer and die.

When I use the term God here, I speak of what feels true to you whether you use the term God, Creator, Higher Power, Source, Lord, Divine, Inner Wisdom, Higher Self, Spirit, Universe, or any other.

One of the most helpful perspectives shared during my darkest days of pain came from the Reverend Christine Robinson during her regular Sunday service sermon. The sermon was not directed at me or solely the circumstance of bereavement, but it felt like a message meant just for me when I desperately needed it. Early on, well-meaning people frequently said to us that "everything happens for a reason." Many newly bereaved people hear this statement. When I had just horribly lost my son in a fiery plane crash, this did not provide comfort or support and felt like another assault. There was no way this tragedy was somehow okay and I felt more comforted because there was a reason for it. And I doubt anyone who said this would feel it was okay or be comforted by this if it was their child who never came home again. At this service, the words Christine said were enlightening. She said, "Rather than understand events in life as everything happens for a reason, perhaps, instead, we can find meaning through the events in our lives." Although my grief was too heavy for this to make me feel a whole lot better when I heard it, it provided a shred of hope that I might make some sense of this thing that felt only cruel and senseless.

Trusting there is something beyond us can help us find some meaning through our child's death. In these five years since Connor died, I have had many people who never met him tell me how much he has impacted their lives. The impact may come from a story I share about his life or an experience I share that I have had after his death. The impact may stem from the profoundness of a poem he wrote when he was just 10 years old describing how we need to "look with clearer eyes" and people need to "make the most of what you have, not what you don't get." When people who never met him feel an impact from his life, my heart warms and I feel greater meaning. When others share that they live in a more authentic and conscious way because of Connor's life and his tragic death, I find some meaning.

Signs from our loved ones in spirit can come in many different forms. When children have passed away, they can be particularly diligent in trying to reach out to parents and siblings to comfort them. The signs and messages are ones of hope and support to show that they truly are well and not suffering regardless of the particular circumstances of their life or death. And they try to give messages of hope for us to know that they feel our pain and take measures to comfort us while walking along side us on this arduous journey.

I devoured many books about the experiences of people who had lost a loved one, and I was astonished at the similarities of the most common signs they received. The experiences were consistent regardless of how different the individual circumstances were. When I sat with groups of other bereaved people at meetings, I heard many similar ways in which their loved ones in spirit were reaching out.

One of the earliest signs for me was one that I had read about and involves the manipulation of electrical frequencies. We are essentially pure energy. Although the physical body may die, our souls never die. We are energy housed in a human body, but our children who have passed are still energy without the physical body. Our loved ones in spirit, being pure energy, can easily manipulate electrical current. These occurrences come in the form of lights going on and off, radio frequencies changing, doorbells ringing, telephones ringing, fans going on and off, etc. Children work very hard to give signs that will be unquestionably familiar to the parents and personally touch their hearts.

There are a few ways you can better trust that you are receiving a sign from your loved one. First, notice if there is any familiarity for you with the sign. As an example, we had a bizarre occurrence the morning after the accident. Shortly before Connor went to Sedona, we had purchased a recently used car for MacKenzie because she had just gotten her driver's license. The car was prominently on my mind that morning since I was more panicked than ever and worried about her safety after the crash that had just taken my son. We talked a lot about the car before Connor went on his trip, and he was very excited because his sister would have her first car and could drive him around. That morning, and out of the blue, the car horn started going off repeatedly. It was so loud that we heard it easily while we were inside the house. This had never happened before, and we all kind of froze and felt it was very odd. We paused, took notice, and wondered aloud whether that could be Connor. It seemed like the horn could be a sign because there was a close connection to what our family had been focused on right before Connor's trip, and Connor was really happy about the car. Also, I had been thinking heavily about whether the car was safe enough for MacKenzie at the moment the horn started going off. We did not go out to the car to fix it or even touch it, but the car horn stopped on its own after we acknowledged it and never went off again.

After Connor's passing, I created a playlist on my iPhone that contained spiritual songs and songs about loss. I could relate to these songs, and they comforted me because they spoke to what was closest on my heart when most other things seemed so irrelevant. Those songs spoke words I could not yet form or find. They spoke to my experience and helped me to feel less alone. When Connor would try to send a sign through a sound on my phone, he would do it when I was playing this list. He would either freeze my phone so that it would stop right in the middle of a particularly relevant set of lyrics, or he would make a sound on the phone during a particularly touching line. Both would get my attention immediately and make me take notice. He did this same thing many times, and there was nothing wrong with my phone. My phone was a new iPhone, and it only jammed or made sounds while I was listening to this playlist and never while playing other songs or playlists.

Although it was easy to question whether these were signs from Connor, I knew they were for a number of reasons. First, this occurrence was connected to Connor and wasn't just random. The songs that were interrupted were always ones that expressed pain or hope. And they always happened during moments when I was most hurting and felt I could not go on. Another way I knew this was a sign from Connor is that it became a pattern that was repeated and there were not physical explanations for these occurrences. The last way I knew this was Connor was that my heart just knew. The key to understanding if you have received a sign, is to ask what your heart feels when you notice the sign. You will know quickly whether your heart feels moved and touched or whether you feel tears. This is your biggest confirmation. It may not be easily explainable to a person on the outside, but if it is a sign from your loved one, your heart will know. If it is not a sign, you will notice the experience physically and analytically but not be touched emotionally or feel it deeply in your heart.

Katie lost her young daughter to a rare form of Leukemia when the girls was just a toddler. Katie wanted to see signs that her daughter was okay and was still near her. People told her about seeing feathers and coins as signs, so she always watched for these. Katie got very excited one day when she stumbled upon three pennies while she was walking from her car to work. When she looked more closely, the three pennies were banged up and quite grubby, and they were partly buried underneath a pile of dirt and leaves. More importantly, she didn't feel anything when she saw them. While Katie wanted badly to think her daughter had sent a sign, it just did not seem like other people had described when they saw one, and she felt it wasn't one.

Katie had also heard about butterflies being a common sign from children who died. One day when she felt particularly sad, she went on an easy hike with her dog. Being in nature always helped her pained heart and relaxed her mind a little. While Katie was hiking and thinking deeply about her daughter, she saw one of the most beautiful monarch butterflies she had ever seen. It repeatedly crossed in front of her, and this brought her such peace. Her heart warmed, and she felt a spark of hope come to her unexpectedly. Katie was very excited as she recognized that her daughter was with her and sending her a message of love. She knew it was a sign because of the way the butterfly kept repeating its pattern so closely in front of her, the way her heart felt when she experienced it, and the unique beauty of this butterfly, which reflected the unique beauty of her daughter.

Another common sign sent by our loved ones in spirit are feathers. Feathers have deep spiritual significance, and our loved ones can send them easily. Stories of people finding feathers left for them in odd places and at odd times were numerous in the books I read, and I experienced this, too.

Our loved ones in spirit also frequently try to let us know they are okay with signs involving insects and birds. I read many accounts of these experiences by other people that mirrored my own. I had received signs from Connor in the form of butterflies, grasshoppers, moths, hummingbirds, doves, and even a praying mantis perched in the middle of my kitchen table when all of my doors and windows were closed and locked. Many of the most beautiful signs I received early on were from butterflies and hummingbirds.

A few weeks after the plane crash, our family went to Sedona. Since none of us had been with Connor, we wanted to find out what they had done while they were there, and we wanted to see for ourselves where the accident happened. A number of the employees at the Sedona Airport, the airport restaurant, and Sky Ranch Lodge helped us tremendously and shared as many details as they knew about the trip. An airport official named Tom was the first responder the morning of the crash, and he helped us immensely on the day we visited. Through very difficult terrain, he escorted us to the crash site, and the four of us spent time there. It was extraordinarily painful to be there, yet there was great peace and natural beauty at this site, too, which was hard to explain. While we sat quietly, we were blessed to experience a number of special and sacred moments in the midst of our deep despair.

I had brought plastic sunflowers and white orchids to place in the hard ground at the base of the crash site, which was 700 feet down in a ravine. The sunflowers were special for Connor because he grew gigantic ones in our garden right before he went on the trip. And the white orchids were representative of his youth, purity, and innocence. After we had dug a hole in the dry dirt and secured the flowers so they would not erode away, a hummingbird came out of nowhere and began to dance around me. This hummingbird moved around me just like the ones on my patio at home earlier. The hummingbird hovered for a while over the sunflowers while looking directly at me. Then it went straight to the white flowers and hovered again while looking directly at me. It then went directly in front of Bryan's face and hovered and locked eyes with him. After that a second hummingbird came out of nowhere, and we watched the two dance and frolic around us, right in front of our faces, before flying off together frolicking more as they went.

A short time later, two large, yellow butterflies came near us and danced back and forth the entire time we were there. They were comforting and looked as if they were playing with one another, darting in and out and up and down with one another. It seemed just like how Connor and Connor messed around with one another and raced each other as is typical for two teenaged boys. This experience brought great peace to our hearts, and we continued to see large, yellow butterflies many times in the years to follow, frequently in two's and always on the anniversary of the accident. During the time we were at the crash site, we were visited by 2 song birds, 2 lizards, 2 hummingbirds, and 2 yellow butterflies, all coming directly to where we sat and spending time near us.

Dr. Elisabeth Kubler-Ross developed the model of the five stages of grief and was a pioneer in near-death studies and hospice treatment. She studied and wrote about the symbolic meaning of butterflies, which she believed represent our eternal souls. Butterflies are particularly significant spiritual symbols of children who have passed away. After visiting a concentration camp, Kubler-Ross discovered that some of the barracks which housed the children had butterflies drawn all over the walls. The children used their fingernails and pebbles to etch the impressions before they were taken away. Kubler-Ross came to believe this was an intuitive knowing by these children that their souls were immortal. Their bodies would die, but they would live on in a different form.

When we think of a caterpillar, we may think its life ends when it goes into the cocoon. Spiritually, the interpretation is that the caterpillar represents our first stage, the cocoon (or death) is only the second stage of transformation, and the butterfly that emerges in the end is the final stage of transformation and the continuation of life in a different, more evolved, and freer form. Dr. Kubler-Ross believed this is why the butterfly was symbolic for the children who faced death in the concentration camps. Intuitively they knew they were continuing life in a different form and would experience an even greater freedom like the butterfly. The butterfly has become the symbol adopted by The Compassionate Friends to represent children who have passed away. An international organization, The Compassionate Friends supports parents, grandparents, and siblings who have survived the loss of a child. It is also symbolic of the parents and siblings as we emerge into something new after the loss of our children.

I told the story earlier of the hummingbirds that visited us regularly and built a nest above my chair on our patio. Hummingbirds also have great spiritual significance. Hummingbirds flap their wings in the pattern of a sideways number 8, which is also known as the infinity sign.

The infinity sign is a comforting one for many bereaved people because it helps us feel that we will always be connected with our loved ones through infinity. When I learned of this remarkable infinity pattern of the hummingbird's wings, it was particularly special for me.

When Connor was seven years old, he made me a homemade coupon book for Mother's Day. It had individual sheets that I could tear out and redeem from him for loving services. One coupon was for two free bed makings. Another coupon was for one back rub. And another coupon was for one free pomegranate "de-seeding." This was funny because I loved pomegranate seeds but didn't like how long it took to take the seeds out of one. Connor was extremely patient, and he loved to do this, so one free de-seeding was a great gift for both of us. The amazing part was the cover. He colored it and wrote, "Happy Mother's Day To Mom, Love Connor." He included an expiration date like you would find on a typical coupon. It said, "Expiration Date, Infinity."

One of our greatest obstacles to seeing a sign from a loved one is our reliance on only left brain processing to understand it. Many cultures process information and understand our world using right brain processing and spiritual perspectives as well. Many advanced, ancient societies understood their worlds using a combination of left and right brain processing and spiritual perspectives. They did not believe that the only things that were real were the ones that could be scientifically analyzed and proven. But often today, especially in many western cultures, we rely heavily or solely on data, science, analytics, and proof. While these are critical, what we can know is not limited to these methods alone.

Before Connor died I shared the perspective that for something to be real I needed to be able to see it and explain it logically supported by facts, science, and proof. But I have grown to understand that the "proof" I've come to know when I receive a sign is in many ways greater. It comes from a significant place of knowing deep inside of me that I hear so much clearer now and is spiritually connected. When I allow my left brain to dominate or give others permission to talk me out of what I think I experienced because I can't prove it, I block an important connection with Connor and with God. This blocking happened a lot in the early days when I would receive signs. I trust myself and my inner wisdom so much more now that this is far less of a problem.

Another obstacle we can face is the fear of creating false hope within ourselves. When I first started to receive signs, it was the greatest hope and joy I had felt in so long after such darkness and pain. At the same time, I felt incredibly scared. It felt risky to open myself up to hope again after my heart had been shattered. I found that I blocked many signs because I was too afraid of more devastation if I allowed myself to hope and it turned out not to be real.

Another issue is difficulty with expression after trauma. Many people lose the ability to fully express themselves after experiencing a traumatic loss. This happened to me. Previously a strong communicator, I had much greater difficulty expressing things after Connor died. The English language did not contain words for me to describe the darkness and pain of the journey that was thrust upon me. It was difficult to share feelings of shame, sorrow, confusion, anger, horror, and terror that were newly real to me. How could I readily share with others what I was now experiencing with Connor when these feelings churning inside me were intense, varied, and complex as I tried to process my new world?

When I speak about signs with another person, it can stir up uncomfortable feelings inside of them and they may shut down. Many of us who are bereaved end up teaching others how to walk through this experience with us. People want to be with us and supportive, but they don't always know how if they have not experienced significant trauma or tragedy themselves. It is a challenging position to be in for the bereaved person because it requires enormous energy and grace, more than we may have available inside. At times my voice was strong enough to speak about my experiences when others found them hard to believe. Other times I was feeling too vulnerable or was still carefully processing them that I could not find a way to share them.

A significant obstacle to trusting in the signs we receive is the confusion between religious practice and spirituality. I have frequently heard people say, "I don't believe in signs because I am not religious." The spiritual connectedness I am referring to has nothing to do with any particular religion. I have known people from many religions and faiths who have received signs and people from those same religions and faiths who have not. I have known people who have no specific religion who receive signs and people with no specific religion who have not seen signs. A person's religious beliefs and practices do not determine the ability to connect with a loved one in spirit or a higher power.

I can honestly say that the moment I started to truly understand and trust that Connor was still with me was the moment I felt life again. I began to realize that there might be a way out of the darkness. I started to feel small moments of hope and see glimpses of a future that might contain light and happiness instead of just the pain that had encompassed me for so long. I could confidently begin to find a new foundation to replace the one that I had carefully built, believed in, and then lost. This foundation was one I had previously thought was secure enough that it could never destruct in the way it did. The new grounding I was exploring and experiencing taught me that if Connor did still exist in a different form and was walking with me through my days, maybe new and beautiful life might be possible for me again.

The greatest discipline I have learned is to slow down and pay attention in our chaotic world. When I got bogged down in the minutia of small things or faced difficult challenges, I would feel that Connor had gone away, and maybe I had imagined it all. Then he would give me a sign of encouragement to go in nature or to be still for a while, and I would find that he had not gone anywhere, and I could still feel his presence. I also had to learn how to use more of all of my senses as I walked through my days. Signs could come through each of them, and he was slowly guiding me to be able to receive more diverse ones.

If you would like to receive signs from your loved one or increase the number you now receive, I invite you to find moments in your day or week that you can slow down and observe more of what is around you. You can make this a practice of walking for 30 minutes each day, or you can save two hours on the weekend to go out in nature. The more regular your practice of slowing down and having quiet time, the more likely you are to see and experience new things. When you expand your awareness of what is all around you, you will begin to experience much more than you may have ever thought possible.

CHAPTER 8

Encouraging More Signs

*"… it's in the way we listen for the messages in the flames
and dig for the treasure in the ashes."*
~ Elizabeth Lesser

Even with the passing of time and the greater comfort I felt from receiving signs, I still ached. I experienced many times when the grief would attack me, and I would feel like I was run over by a truck again. Many things are grief triggers, and it is amazing how quickly one can take me back to the deepest feelings of despair that Connor is not physically here with me. The trigger can be large and obvious like

April 27, 2016, which would have been Connor's 18th birthday when he would have reached adulthood and graduated high school a month later with all of his friends. But it can also be smaller and unexpected like when I walk past a young man of 14 or 15, and he smells of the same Axe body wash scent that Connor used.

This intense ache also occurs when I hear lovely piano music. MacKenzie, Connor, and Erin all played the piano beautifully starting at a young age, a blessing and gift for which Bryan and I were always grateful. Connor had a passion for composing songs on the piano. He won composition contests for creating original compositions starting when he was just seven years old. He loved to sit for hours at the piano and compose music. Much of it he never recorded or wrote down as it just flowed out of him, and he was happy being in the moment. When I hear someone play like this, it will take me back in an instant to the gaping hole that was suddenly created on July 26, 2012, when we never heard his music again.

What balanced these continued experiences of pain that were often present was the comfort I received through signs. As time passed the frequency, consistency, and number of signs I received increased. When I began to question their validity a lot less and trust in them more, I craved learning as much as I could about them. I began to read anything that I could find about the topic. It can sound a little "woo-woo" to say that I researched signs and messages from the afterlife, but it is astonishing how much has been written on the topic. Many people from all cultures have had near-death experiences or miraculous interventions from the Divine. There are so many accounts of the afterlife that have been written by individuals who have had these experiences and by both current and historical spiritual teachers. I read a number of books by doctors and scientists who survived near-death incidents and shared their stories of what they experienced. In each case, they did not previously believe these experiences were possible because they were medically and scientifically trained to believe in only the things that could be proven. After their profound experiences, they lived with greatly altered perspectives and understandings that they applied to both their personal and professional lives. Once I began talking about this and looking for others who had experiences like I had, it was astonishing to find how many there were. As James Van Praagh said, "Signals from spirit can be elaborate or simple, but they are always around us."

Through different sources I had been introduced to the idea that we can encourage more signs from our loves ones in spirit. I did not know anybody who had tried this, and the thought had not occurred to me previously that we might influence the signs we receive. I definitely wanted to learn more and decided to try the practices I read about to see whether it was possible. Surprisingly, I discovered I could influence the signs I received and began receiving them more often. It seemed to work the following way:

- Create more open space and still time
- Ask your loved one or your sense of God / Source / Creator to send you a sign
- Express gratitude from your heart for the sign when you receive it
- Ask for clarity of a sign or ask for it to be repeated when you are unsure
- Ask to receive signs more frequently and express more gratitude when you do

The first place to start if you want to encourage signs from your loved ones is to create open space and expand your awareness so that you can notice and interpret more. We can limit our ability to receive signs because we think only of one or two senses. Perhaps we only consider signs we can see or hear. It's possible to receive signs using all of the senses depending on our awareness and practice. But it takes having your mind and senses quieted and calmed for small periods of time each day so that you can become aware of them. Our loved ones in spirit are sending signs, but we may not notice them as we rush through our days and stay centered on our busy schedules.

Asking for a sign can be one of the most important steps to receiving one. In situations when a loss is traumatic, such as the loss of a child, a tragic accident, a suicide, or a murder, our loved ones will reach out to us with signs of connection and love to reassure us. But we may be in so much deep pain that it is hard for us to recognize them. We need to ask for signs. You can ask for a general sign that your loved one is still with you and is at peace, or you can ask for a sign to give you guidance about something specific. Asking expresses your open desire to receive signs, and you will receive more when you do. There are times I have asked for signs of comfort when I am experiencing a particularly painful time. Other times I have asked for a sign to reinforce an intuition I had or something particular I was wondering about. I have also asked for a sign about which path to follow when presented with multiple options. In each of these cases, I have received the signs and have grown over time to be better able to interpret and trust them.

While writing this book I started to share more stories with friends and colleagues about my experiences asking for and receiving signs. There were times when a person respected my experiences but did not really believe this was possible. Many times the same person would come back to me a short time later and share a beautiful story of surprisingly receiving a sign. The person may have asked for a sign from one of their loved ones in spirit, or they may have asked Connor for a sign to show them what I was saying was real. Each time they received a beautiful sign after asking, and they were changed by the experience. Many asked for a second sign still not believing or trusting the first sign, and another clear sign quickly followed to affirm the first one. A couple of acquaintances of mine received signs from Connor even when they had never met him.

My friend, Michelle, had never met Connor. Our families knew one another, but we did not meet until the fall after Connor was killed. While she was very compassionate to our family, she wasn't sure she could believe that signs from our loved ones were possible. After reading this book, she was supportive but still doubtful. We talked about it, and a short time later she told me the following story:

"I struggled while reading the book with the idea of a spiritual connection and signs – wanting to believe but feeling unsure and even skeptical. So I opened my heart one morning and asked Connor for a sign to help me understand. Later that evening on a walk with my husband we saw a magnificent double rainbow. I had not even noticed it since it was behind us until a woman driving by pointed enthusiastically to it. I thought to myself, 'Maybe this is Connor with a sign,' but then thought I might be searching too hard for signs. As I stood watching and thinking about Connor and signs, something made me look down at the ground below the rainbows. I saw one pristine feather standing straight up in the rocks, all by itself, simple and profound. I felt it in my heart and I knew. I was filled with gratitude and joy, thankful for all the possibilities and joyful to have finally met Connor."

People may ask their loved one in spirit for signs, and others may ask God or their Higher Power for signs. This depends very much on the individual connection each person has with what is outside of the physical world around us. Signs can regularly come from the Divine and not a specific loved one in spirit, and signs can come from a loved one in spirit and not from your sense of God or the Universe. Having one of these connections can lead to creating a connection with the other. One friend of mine has always received signs from God but never received them from the child she lost. After exploring these possibilities more and asking her child for signs, she now receives signs from both. A fellow bereaved parent regularly received signs from her child who died but did not receive signs from her Higher Power. After asking and learning about different ways to receive signs, she now experiences signs from both. Whatever the source of your signs or messages the path is sacred, and this experience can give you profound and needed guidance for greater healing and living more meaningfully.

Expressing gratitude when we receive a sign is important because it opens the door to receiving more. It also lets our loved one in spirit know that we are grateful for the signs and that they make a difference to us. This might seem like it would be obvious but it is important. I noticed personally that the more frequently I expressed gratitude and the more deeply I expressed it from my heart, the more signs that followed. I particularly express strong gratitude when I receive a sign that is funny or really unexpected since I usually need a lift at that time. Connor was very funny in life, and he loved to tease me. He was good at helping me lighten up when I would get too serious. His signs now are often funny ones or ones that make me laugh at myself or what I am doing at that moment. I have grown to be able to feel Connor's sense of humor similarly in spirit as I could when he was here physically. This is lovely and truly a blessing.

Signs and messages can be answers to our prayers or our requests for help. We do not always recognize them as this for two reasons. The first reason is that the sign or message might come at a later time, and we don't connect the sign back to what we asked for help with earlier. If I receive a sign but cannot make the immediate connection of what it might mean, I have learned to pause and think back to what I asked for help with or requested guidance on recently. I can make the connection more easily when I pause to reflect on the decisions I am trying to make in my life or the particular pain I am dealing with at that time.

The second reason we might not recognize a sign, and one of the most important, is that answers to our prayers can come in a different form than we expect. We may not realize it, but we usually have a preconceived notion of what the answer should be or the one we want. And when we do not get just that, we think our prayers were never answered. At other times we may not like the answer we receive, so we don't accept it. I have learned that the answers I like least are usually the ones I need the most, and they are indeed still signs and messages to help me.

I found that most people believed my experiences and understood what I was discovering. I was surprised and grateful when I learned that others had these experiences, too. But this new way of thinking and believing challenged the ideas of other people I knew including some of my closest loved ones. Those people felt this was just desperate reaching by a mother in pain, and they encouraged me to "move on." They distanced from me after the immediacy passed. What I experienced most often was that when I was willing to share my new experiences, others opened up and wanted to share theirs, too. I found many more people who believed these experiences were possible and who were anxious to learn more about them and share ones of their own than I did people who were closed to these possibilities.

While the very first signs and messages I received were simple signs for momentary comfort, I have come to find much deeper meaning through the messages I receive now. I have developed a new relationship with Connor and have an expanded spiritual connection with God as well. Signs can come in many ways, and I receive them from Connor through all of my senses.

There may be one or two favorite signs or messages you receive that are special and particularly meaningful to you and your loved one. For a long time, yellow butterflies and feathers were my most common and special signs from Connor. One of my clients receives signs of hummingbirds, songs, and pennies the most. When we expand our awareness and ask for more signs and messages, we can begin to receive them in more diverse ways. Special ones may then emerge for you and your loved one. If you would like to expand your ability to receive more signs, information is provided at the end of the book for you to learn more.

CHAPTER 9

Fostering Changes for Deeper Living

"The quieter you become, the more you can hear."

~ Ram Dass

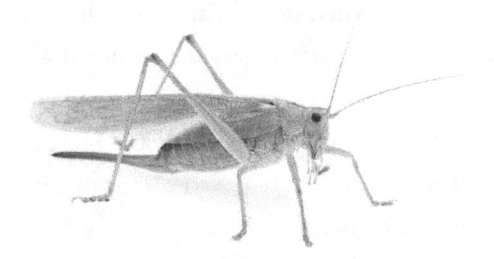

A round the three-year anniversary I started to feel a small but significant shift. I noticed that the proportion of time each day that I felt the darkness was lessening, and the proportion that I was feeling connected to Connor and to my life again was increasing. The amount of time I was feeling more hopeful was a little greater, too. The waves and experiences of grief still wiped me out and knocked me down intensely when they came. Sometimes it took a while to get back up. But the balance of feeling more and more connected to Connor and grounded in a new foundation of spiritual significance inspired me to dig deeper. I wanted more of the hope and less of the pain. Although people would comment about time passing and say they could see time helping me heal, I knew that it was more than time. Walking through my ashes and feeling all the pain that needed to be felt was the first and ongoing part. The second part was doing the hard work of opening to this new life and awakening to what I could learn. I could sense that bigger changes would help expand what I was learning, and my desire to increase my connectedness further gave me greater courage to try more.

I mentioned earlier the new activities I began that started to open up space for something new. These included practicing yoga and meditation, increasing the number of times and ways in which I consciously expressed gratitude, spending more time in nature, allowing small spaces each day to just be still, and including prayer in my life in a more meaningful and heartfelt way. I continued all of these practices but wondered more about why these were so helpful. Learning had already helped me along this grief journey and increased my trust in the transformation I was experiencing. As I did at previous points, I began to search for more information.

One of the things I learned more about was our energy. Our loved ones in spirit are pure energy as we are inside of our human bodies. But in spirit our loved ones have an infinitely stronger and higher frequency of this energy. When we feel the presence of a loved one who has passed away, we experience this presence as a vibrational frequency. We can increase our spiritual connection by raising our frequency. Much has been written about ways to raise your vibrational frequency, and the new activities I had incorporated were the very things that helped. Activities that were particularly helpful for this were prayer, yoga, meditation, a focus on gratitude, positive affirmations, and health practices like acupuncture and using essential oils. These actions shift our energy from the left brain to the right brain and create new levels of frequency inside of us to raise our vibration. I could see how the changes I had made helped me do this and allowed me to become more connected to Connor and God.

There was not a day when I made a formal goal to increase my vibration. This just started to happen more organically and slowly with the changes I had made. I began to practice yoga on a regular basis because I really enjoyed it and felt more grounded and relaxed when I did. Yoga reduced my stress, and I had greater clarity on major questions I was facing. During yoga I began to experience more signs and messages, so I kept a pen and pad of paper near me to jot quick notes for later reflection. I would have multiple or significant ones that were answers to my prayers or helpful guidance on the decisions I was facing in my life. The more I deepened my yoga, meditation, and general relaxation practices, the more powerful the signs and answers to my prayers became.

In addition to yoga and meditation, I deepened my gratitude practice and could feel how this changed my energy level and raised my vibration. It also gave me a surprising new tool to replace unhealthy coping habits with a new healthy one. Whenever I got too sad and low missing Connor, I could raise myself up more quickly by journaling about the things I was grateful for or listing these things out loud. When I was sad or angry and felt like reaching for an extra glass of wine or a large bag of chips that would leave me with a stomach ache, I found that expressing gratitude changed my thoughts and built new energy. I could recover from these low times more quickly, and I received supportive and comforting signs because my vibration was higher.

More and more I started turning to these new practices. I was committed to doing yoga in the early mornings before work. Very early morning was not my first choice of times as it was still hard each morning to get myself out of bed and face the day. But I was more likely to practice yoga if I did it before my day started, and I found that my connectedness to my inner wisdom and divine guidance was so much greater at this early hour, too.

My struggles with meditation took a long time to improve. I knew the key was mindfulness, but that was still difficult with my mourning. It was a beautiful breakthrough when I noticed I was getting better and better at relaxation and meditation, even if it was just for short periods of time. I also worked this into my day before work. It was tough each morning to pull myself out of bed at 5:00 or 5:30 to do this, but the payoff was always wonderful, and it pushed me to do it again the next day and the next until it became easier and more of a habit.

Prayer was a really big change for me. I had never understood prayer well until after Connor died. It just didn't seem to work for me, and I was not able to feel the special feeling that people who "got it" described. At one point early on, I asked my grief counselor about prayer. I told Dr. Hopkins I just did not understand it but desperately wanted to. At the memorial service and in the early months after, so many people offered me prayers that were deep from their hearts. I wanted this to be as meaningful for me to receive as it was for them to give. But I could not feel it like that. I just wanted my son back not prayers. I asked Dr. Hopkins to tell me what I was doing wrong and teach me how to do it so I felt it like others did. As I felt rather silly saying this, he kindly reassured me that many other people have felt the same way. He said he had moments when he had felt that way, too. He told me I just needed to speak from my heart about what was real. There was not a right way or a wrong way to pray, and I could not offend God or ask too much from God. Dr. Hopkin's words were encouraging. He also said that it might take time of speaking the words before I felt anything behind them. What he said was true for me. It took time, but things did begin to change for me after I kept with it. I did begin to feel like I was connected to God and Connor when I prayed and that things grew in me as I did. It was quite a beautiful feeling to experience after so many years without it.

Dreams were the next area of spiritual deepening and awareness for me. Usually, I either did not dream because I was so tired by the time I dropped into bed, or I did not remember what I dreamt. I remembered the constant nightmares in the early months when I kept searching everywhere for Connor but could never find him. And then I remember the sporadic beautiful dreams of Connor and powerful visitations that helped me choose to go on during my darkest of times. The rest of the time just felt blank during my sleep.

The most unusual thing began to happen to me. I did not take much notice at first, but it was another experience that I realized was forming a pattern over time. Regardless of what time I went to bed, I awoke between 3:00 a.m. and 5:00 a.m., and most usually this was right around 4:00. The experience was curious because it felt like I was being pulled out of my sleep. Once awake I could not identify an obvious reason for waking up such as needing to use the bathroom, hearing a noise, or one of my daughters needing me. What I did realize was that I had always woken straight from a dream. While I typically could not remember much of the dream offhand, I started to write them down. I didn't really want to wake myself up further to write because usually all I could remember at that moment was a jumble of crazy images. But I decided to follow my instinct and write down whatever I had seen or felt and what was running around in my head. I kept a journal and pen right next to my bedside and even got creative about how to minimally sit up to write and turn on as little light as possible so I could more easily go back to sleep afterward.

What was remarkable was there were always messages in my dreams, and they frequently came in the form of intricate and meaningful metaphors. They tended to be answers to my prayers or messages of hope about the things that were worrying me. There were messages encouraging me to seek out new steps I was considering but feared. I realized I was receiving a beautiful gift from the Divine because the messages were helping steer my life in new, healthy directions. I always expressed sincere gratitude for what I received, and writing down the dreams helped me to receive more and more. They increased to the point that they happened every night. On certain nights I was too tired to write, but most nights I did record my vivid dreams because the insight I received through them was so helpful and miraculous. Through the process of writing, I remembered a lot more detail, and the metaphors emerged to reveal far deeper meaning. Over time my ability to recognize messages through metaphors presented to me during the daytime improved, too. Some important changes I initiated in my life came from the divine guidance and supportive messages I received within those dreams, and every one of them improved my life in beautiful ways I could not have imagined.

I found many interesting and comforting books along my journey. One comforting book I read early on was *How to Heal a Grieving Heart* by Doreen Virtue and James Van Praagh. It contained beautiful images and perspectives about the passing of a loved one that were hopeful and healing. Another helpful book I received as a gift was *Angel Numbers 101.* This book described the meaning of numbers when we received them as signs. Especially meaningful numbers were those with a digit repeated multiple times such as 333, 444, or 111. Also significant were ones with twice repeated digits such as 33, 22, or 88. Although I did not think I ever saw numbers like this before, I could not believe how regularly meaningful numbers were presented to me once I took notice. I had read and saw for myself that number messages could come on a digital clock, a number on a receipt, the digital temperature on a building sign, the miles on a car, license plate numbers, or telephone numbers. The key that makes a unique number significant or a sign is what is taking place or being thought about at the moment when the number is seen. There is a connection between what is happening or being thought about at the time and what the number symbolizes. Typically, people will say that "something" just made them look down or up at that moment, and the number was there.

Like most of my other experiences, I felt unsure and awkward at first talking with others about how my new awareness and these experiences were transforming my life. It was not what anyone I knew had talked about. As was the case with many of my prior experiences, once I spoke about this with others, I was surprised how many people had experienced this same thing and followed the guidance from these number messages. This was true even with people in different locations and from other cultures. I also found that much had been researched and written about this very phenomenon. People who I never would have expected shared very powerful stories with me about these same types of experiences.

During the times that my trust and faith were weak, I doubted my experiences and yearned for hard and fast "proof." I had lived many years relying on left brain processing and following cultural norms of what was considered "real." It was a difficult pattern to change. Worrying about what others thought of this new path I did not yet fully understand burdened me a little. At times I felt like I lived in a one-dimensional world part of my day and in a multi-dimensional one that many others could not see the other part of my day. There were times the answer to a prayer that I received was not the one I wanted. And other times I did not always like the answer. These could be blocks for me or opportunities. Most of the time when I did not like or want a particular sign or answer, I asked for better clarity and understanding about it. Usually I received it, and then I could better understand and more easily accept the message.

As I reflect back to my earliest steps on this relentless and dark path of grief, I recall the first tool bag I created. It was interesting to see how a few simple early comforts transformed into substantial growth tools that had greater purpose. That initial set of life-saving soothers such as coffee, baths, and comforting music transformed into a set of practices that increased my vibration. I discovered that we have great power to increase our vibration, which can bring a greater connection with our loved ones and God.

The more I have deepened my practices, the greater I influence how much connectedness I feel and the signs I can receive. With a higher vibration, I have received help with everyday challenges and questions as well as guidance about the bigger questions in my life. I understand better what my purpose is and where I should go next. Feeling more connected with Connor, I have developed a new relationship with him that I had never thought possible. Knowing he has not abandoned me, which is how it felt for a long time, is wondrous and beautiful. And it has given me signs of true hope and inspiration that there is meaning and light I can find through this profound loss. This idea is what the Reverend Christine Robinson referred to early on - finding new meaning through my loss - which at the time I could only wish longingly to be possible.

CHAPTER 10

Healing & a New Spiritual Foundation

"In the difficult are the friendly forces, the hands that work on us."
~ Rainer Maria Rilke

No matter when you have picked up this book, you may still have great pain and a life that feels very dark. Even though you may want nothing more than to have your child back, you have been taking steps within this new life that no longer includes your child. It may feel like happiness, hope, faith, and wholeness are far away, and you cannot see the path to them. You want to feel in control of your life again and would like to identify any meaning through this terrible experience you have been living.

It is possible for you to open to a new process that provides a connection to your child or loved one. You can learn to see signs that your loved one is not gone and is still with you even as you experience life without him or her physically present. This awareness can bring you greater hope than you have felt in a long time and awaken you to profoundly deeper meaning.

Through acknowledging your new life, you can make conscious decisions about how you live your life going forward and the beliefs that fuel and sustain you on the path. This step is a foundation for creating a life of hope and meaning from the new one you have been given. Parts of this work is quiet and internal, and other parts are more active and external. It requires looking closely at many of the unanswered questions you may have surrounding God and any possible meaning you understand through your loss.

By giving yourself permission for new things in your life and creating new rituals that better fit now, you begin to acknowledge the new person inside that is emerging. You are not the same person you were before your loss, and many old ways that once fit well may no longer serve you. Finding new hope and happiness requires knowing more about the parts of you that remain and the parts of you that are different since the death of your child. While it can feel painful to think you may lose anything more, recognizing and honoring the new person you are becoming is important. You can choose to align the things in your life that take your time and energy with the new life you are experiencing, even if you did not want it.

Creating space for something new can feel awkward and uncertain. You may question what value there is in this when you may not care much about your new world. You can find the courage to let go of people, experiences, routines, and activities that drain you more than they serve you. Otherwise, these activities distract from the painful but important work of learning to create a life without your child or loved one present, which requires full energy every day.

Learning to see signs from your child and feeling that your child is still with you is inspiring, beautiful, and can create the hope you desperately need. You can learn to use all of your senses to receive signs. You can learn to hear with your heart and intuition to know that your child or loved one is supporting, comforting, and guiding you. Our loved ones are ready and available to help us if we wish. We can feel a deepening of connection and meaning when we begin to trust and have faith that our loved ones have not left us. Seeing signs from your loved one is one of the strongest building blocks of your new foundation. It is also one of the most sacred and rewarding pieces of this new life.

You can go beyond waiting to receive signs sporadically to taking steps that help you receive more and clearer signs. You can then make conscious lifestyle changes that help you live more deeply and fully after loss. New healthy habits such as yoga, meditation, prayer, and gratitude practices shift our energy from the left brain to the right brain and create new levels of frequency inside of us to raise our vibration. These changes, which feel wonderful on their own, also help you to experience more signs. You can feel more positive about everything in your life even as the pain of loss continues. When you regularly encourage and receive more signs, you will find you receive greater guidance as well. This can help you with practical aspects of your everyday life as well as larger decisions about how you live this new life going forward. As you deepen your connection with your child, you may find new meaning and awareness through your loss. You may even find a new or strengthened connection with God that provides a different way of understanding your life and what you have survived.

Through trust and openness, you can find as strong of a connection with your loved one as I have with Connor. This connection can give you new perspective, greater peace, and stronger faith that aids your healing. You will feel less pain of separation when you develop a new relationship with your child in spirit and know this is possible.

I hope my story helps you know there is someone else who comprehends your pain and supports your steps toward happiness again. In sharing my experience, I want to provide comfort, new possibilities, and renewed hope that life can be meaningful and contain beauty again after loss. I desire for you to feel competent and confident again while finding your full voice that speaks new truths with renewed faith. It is my wish that you begin to see more miracles each day alongside your grief.

Although I would still choose to have Connor here to grow up beside me, I feel blessed to have grown and learned so much through him since he cannot be here. I honor and cherish this awakening and am grateful for the new spiritual foundation that has bloomed from it. This foundation supports me and has led to peace and comfort from my deepened spiritual awareness and connection. The Buddha said, "Just as a candle cannot burn without fire, men cannot live without a spiritual life." I will continue to take steps to see where this new consciousness leads me and how I can use it to best honor Connor and help others. Through our own healing, we can transform our pain into something good and better serve our world. I invite you to join me.

Please share your experiences of signs from your loved ones. Many people have these experiences but may not have the openness or opportunity to talk about them. I have found that when I share my experiences, I learn of so many people who were waiting for an invitation to share theirs.

If you want to learn more or talk further about how to deepen your connection with your child or loved one in spirit, please contact me.

There are many ways I can help support you along your journey toward renewed hope, enhanced peace, and greater healing.

A FEATHER SHARED

"Matter is spirit moving slow enough to be seen."
~ Pierre Teilhard de Chardin

Shortly before the four-year anniversary of the plane crash, Connor would have had his 18th birthday and graduated from high school. The following fall my two daughters and I moved for a semester to Italy so they could attend study abroad programs in Milan and Rome. During the spring before moving there, I went to Rome to locate and secure an apartment. Following my week in Rome, I attended a program in Grosseto, Tuscany to write this book.

The formidable nature of this task strongly hit me the morning after I arrived in Grosseto. While I wanted to help others who were facing similar sorrow through sharing my experiences as others had shared with me, I was very nervous and had waves of grief on the morning I was to start. Reliving my story was very painful, and it was difficult for me to share the most heart-shattering experience of my life as well as some of the most sacred experiences to follow. I pretty much wanted to slip away and just forget the idea.

While walking outside to the other side of the house in the early morning to begin writing, I found a beautiful colored feather right in the middle of my path. I smiled and expressed a big heartfelt thank you for this. Earlier that morning I had asked Connor for a very clear sign to help me feel his presence, feel his support, and let me know that I was doing the right thing. I had not found a single feather during my entire time in Italy, but one lay right outside the door of the room where I would begin writing after I had just asked for one. A feather was one of the first signs I received that helped me open to the idea of a continued presence and spiritual connection with Connor. Now it was the sign I received to help me share with others the possibility of a continued presence and connection with their loved ones in spirit. As had usually been the case, the sign came just when I needed it most. And this feather was one of the most beautiful and unique ones I had yet received.

Grosseto, Tuscany, Italy; June 24, 2016

"I need a sign to let me know you're here.
'Cause my TV set just keeps it all from being clear.
I want a reason for the way things have to be.
I need a hand to help build up some kind of hope inside of me."
And I'm calling all angels.
And I'm calling all you angels."

~ "Calling All Angels" by Train

Connor O'Loughlin Mantsch
Pegosa Springs, CO; July 3, 2012

Connor's Memorial Bench at Sky Ranch Lodge; Sedona, AZ

ORIGIN OF THE TITLE;

Life from the Ashes

Connor died in an airplane crash, so perhaps the title seems obvious. There is a deeper meaning to it as well. We were driving home from a family vacation when Connor was ten years old. As we drove through an area that had a recent forest fire, the trees on one side of the road were burned to the ground while the woods on the opposite side stood pristine. I commented aloud that it made me sad to see how beautiful the forest was on the side that was untouched and how desolate it looked on the burned side. Connor loved knowledge and facts and was always full of uncommon pieces of information. He happily shared that when a forest burns down it is actually at its healthiest point and would be nourished with new seeds that would grow to replenish it. He enthusiastically told me never to be sad about seeing this because the forest that grows after the fire will be healthier, stronger, and even more beautiful than the one that existed before.

ACKNOWLEDGMENTS

I am eternally grateful for my son, Connor, who gave me over 14 beautiful years in this life and continues to walk with me every day.

I am eternally grateful for my daughters, MacKenzie and Erin, who are a joy to parent and call my family. Together, with Connor, these three children were my perfect package that I have always felt so very blessed to parent.

I am grateful to Bryan for creating this loving and beautiful family with me.

I am grateful to God for the spiritual connection I now feel in a way that I never before imagined was possible. I am grateful for all of the guidance, love, and support I have received and for the many miracles I have experienced as I have navigated this painful journey.

I am grateful for my extended family who showed up for something no one ever wants to be asked to do and who walked with us through our earliest and darkest days. I am especially grateful to my sisters, Laurie O'Loughlin and Cathy O'Loughlin, and to my uncle Bill O'Loughlin.

I am grateful to all of our incredible friends who gave so much of themselves. I am especially thankful to Joetta Alcalde, Mary Hobbs, Lyndi Spears, Anne Salopek, Matt Salopek, Lisa Hendrix, Lisa Sheedy, Kris Langkammer, Lisa Jansen, Lee Ann Llamas, Sylvia Ho, Diane Ogawa, Jane Cody, Catherine Simpson, Rhonda Thomas, Nora Zulick, Trish Nickerson, Heather Fowler, Gail Hopkins, Gurudarshan Khalsa,

Christine Baca, Gene Baca, Cliff Ho, Tim Spears, Jeff Alcalde, Robert Hobbs, Dean Whitley, Tom Holtz, and Jamie Wilke.

I am grateful to Dr. Paul Hopkins, who gracefully supported me through so many crossroads and very dark days.

I am grateful to Trish Porter for lending me her faith when I did not have any.

I am grateful to the Morgan James Publishing team: Special thanks to David Hancock, CEO & Founder for believing in me and my message. To my Author Relations Manager, Gayle West, thanks for making the process seamless and easy and for being so compassionate and helpful. Many more thanks to everyone else, but especially Jim Howard, Bethany Marshall, and Nicole Watkins.

I am grateful to Angela Lauria & her Author Incubator team, especially Cynthia Kane and Jenn McRobbie, and The Difference Press. I am grateful for my Grosseto author cohorts, Caroline Greene, Cassie Parks, Jill Angie and Sharon Pope for their support, wisdom, and expertise.

I am grateful to Carl Brooks, JJ Van Zon, Diana Torros, Jennifer Lang, Katerina Suplie, Natalie Scott, and Paula Alonso who provided so much encouragement, support, and camaraderie, and who helped me find my voice and courage.

I am grateful to Connor for teaching me about forest fires years ago, so I would know that from the ashes something healthy, strong, and even more beautiful can grow.

ABOUT THE AUTHOR

Shari O'Loughlin has an MBA and 25 years of management and executive experience helping corporations, new businesses, and nonprofits grow. A certified life and business coach, she is President of Shari O'Loughlin Coaching & Consulting. Shari started her own business following her previous role as Chief Operating Officer of a New Mexico technology company. She currently serves as an organizational consultant, growth strategist, business and career coach, and speaker with expertise in helping companies and professionals navigate transition, loss, and change.

Shari believes that we can find new beauty, transformation, and profound meaning from our most traumatic experiences. Learning to find what is on the other side of loss and tragedy helps us lead the lives we truly desire in a deeply meaningful and joyful way. Shari brings her experience as a business executive, leadership trainer, entrepreneur, joyful mother of three, bereaved parent, and bereaved sibling to help others who are experiencing loss identify new possibilities. She combines practical expertise and business acumen with deep compassion, intuition, and wisdom for innovative solutions. Shari masterfully helps others dream, design, and consciously create more powerful and meaningful lives. She helps them transform their pain of loss into new possibilities following bereavement, tragedy, corporate transition, financial devastation, business or job loss, health crisis, and divorce. Shari earned her MBA from the University of Chicago and her BA from the University of Wisconsin-Madison. Originally from the Midwest, Shari and her family live in Albuquerque, New Mexico.

THANK YOU

I am honored that you read my story and shared my transformational journey of hope, spiritual connection, and healing.

As a special thank you, I want to offer my *Path to Healing Care Kit*, which will aid your steps in healing and deepen your understanding on this journey. Exploring these ideas further can help you connect with your loved one in spirit. You can learn to recognize the many ways in which you can receive signs to know that your child or loved one is still with you and reaches out to you with love.

I am offering these free guides and exercises so you can create a beautiful life of meaning and hope that includes your loved one even after your loss. In addition, I offer you a free conversation to discuss the exercises, your personal journey, and how you can have a stronger connection with your child and God to find meaning through your loss.

PATH TO HEALING CARE KIT

- Shifting Perspectives for Deeper Understanding
- Redefining You
- New Rituals & Practices for Healing
- Ways We Can Experience Signs
- Free 30-minute Compassionate Consultation

Please visit www.ShariOLoughlin.com/gift to claim your free *Path to Healing Care Kit* that will aid your grief and healing journey.

Morgan James
Speakers Group

www.TheMorganJamesSpeakersGroup.com

We connect Morgan James published
authors with live and online events
and audiences who will benefit
from their expertise.

Morgan James makes all of our titles available
through the Library for All Charity Organization.

www.LibraryForAll.org